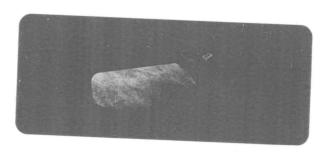

Toni Morrison's World of Fiction

Toni Morrison's World of Fiction

by
Karen Carmean

The Whitston Publishing Company
Troy, New York
1993

Acknowledgements

I would like to thank my colleagues at Converse College for their encouragement and support during this project.

My special thanks goes to Georg Gaston, whose help throughout the whole project was invaluable.

I am also grateful to Toni Morrison for her kind permission to quote from her novels in this study.

Contents

Chapter 1

Introduction

Toni Morrison has said that she "never planned to be a writer."[1] The closest her ambitions took her to a creative life was an early dream of becoming a dancer. But her destiny was writing, even if she didn't know it for a long time. Finally, in her late thirties, she found that writing was not only pleasurable but also necessary for her. Prior to starting her writing career Morrison was increasingly bothered by the feeling that life had somehow passed her by. "I used to really belong in this world," she thought to herself, but "at some point I didn't belong here anymore."[2] The experience of working on her first novel changed all that. As she poured her imagination into her story, and the characters took on life, she became aware of the miraculous rewards of the creative act. "I was everybody," she discovered. "And I fell in love with myself. I reclaimed myself and the world."[3] Moreover, she discovered that writing "was a way of knowing, a way of thinking" that she found "really necessary."[4] Since then, guided by these feelings, Morrison has gone on to write so impressively that she is now recognized as one of the foremost novelists of her time.

Morrison was born Chloe Anthony Wofford on February 18, 1931, in Lorain, Ohio, the second of four children. Both her parents had arrived in this steel mill town on the banks of Lake Erie from the South. Since they happened to be black, they thought of the South not as home but as a region from which they had escaped. Morrison's father had left Georgia because of racist atrocities which haunted him all his life. Thus he became a racist himself, believing he was justified in hating all whites, and holding out no hope that the general lot of his people would improve in this country. Her mother, by contrast, was far more optimistic, believing that faith and individual effort could change conditions. This split between pessimism and hope about the racial situation in America reflected exactly the views of the maternal grandparents. They had migrated to Lorain looking for a better life just like their future son-in-law. Growing up at the time of the Emancipation Proclamation, Morrison's grandfather saw his hopes for the future crushed when he lost his land at the turn of the century and was forced to become a sharecropper, though his wife continued to believe that progress could be achieved through religious and personal faith. Both shared the view, however, that the pursuit of education, if based on a strong sense of values and personal worth, was a key to a better life. This view the grandparents passed on to Morrison's parents, who passed it on to their daughter. Thus, while Morrison remembers growing up in a basically racist home that invited her to hold more than a child's share of contemptuous distrust of white people, she also remembers the great encouragement she received for building her character and mind.[5]

This was a household which also encouraged Morrison's imagination to grow, especially in the vein of black culture. Folk music suffused the house. Morrison's mother took pleasure in singing constantly. Her grandfather played the violin, well enough to have been a professional earlier in life. Folk superstitions, rituals, and lore also played an exciting part in the family's existence. Morrison's grandmother kept a dream book, whose symbols she decoded for playing the numbers. Her parents were gifted story-tellers who impressed on their children the value of the family history and the vitality of their people's language. In a lighter mood, they enjoyed thrilling their children with scary ghost stories. All this Morrison absorbed, so that, when she finally started writing, her rich family heritage played an inspiring role in her fiction.

Early in her life, Morrison was also encouraged to read. As a result, by the time she entered the first grade, the only member of her race in the class, she was the only child who could already read. For the rest of her school years, she remained studious, and her academic accomplishments grew. In 1949 she graduated with honors from Lorain High School. By then she had developed a great passion for reading literature. Jane Austen, Gustav Flaubert, and the great nineteenth-century

Russian novelists in particular had captured her imagination. "These books," she recalls, "were not written for a little black girl in Lorain, Ohio, but they were so magnificently done that I got them anyway—they spoke directly to me out of their own specificity."[6] Thus, she adds, "when I wrote my first novel years later, I wanted to capture that same specificity about the nature and feeling of the culture I grew up in."[7]

After graduating from high school, she decided to pursue her education, specifically her love of literature, at Howard University in Washington, D. C. Her father helped pay her expenses by managing to work at three jobs simultaneously, including his main one of skilled shipyard welder. At Howard, she chose to major in English literature, and she also chose to change her name from Chloe to Toni. After receiving her B. A. in English in 1953, she went on to Cornell University for graduate work. There she earned her M. A. in 1955, having written a thesis which explored the theme of suicide in Faulkner and Virginia Woolf. Now it was time to start her career in teaching, a career she then thought would be life-long. For her first teaching job, Morrison went to Texas Southern University in Houston. But when a little over a year later she had an opportunity to go back to Howard, she jumped at the chance. At Howard, as an instructor in English and the humanities, she had a variety of professional responsibilities. They included teaching general composition, holding literature classes, and being the faculty advisor to the English Club. A gifted teacher, she left her imprint on more than her share of students, including such young luminaries as Stokeley Carmichael, Houston Baker, and Claude Brown. The latter one day took Morrison aback when he hauled in an 800 page manuscript for her to read. This turned out to be the original manuscript of a modern classic, *Manchild in the Promised Land*. Although her professional life kept her very busy, Morrison still felt somehow unfulfilled. Thus, she joined a group of fiction writers and poets who held monthly meetings. All participants were encouraged to share their latest writings for discussions. For a while, Morrison could bring herself only to share some items she had produced in high school. Finally, though, she found herself without her old material, and so she quickly wrote a story about a little black girl's wish for blue eyes. Little did she know this story would eventually serve as the germ of her first novel, and that this was actually the beginning of her writing life.

There had been another significant beginning in her life about this time. Soon after returning to Howard University, Toni met Harold Morrison, a Jamaican architecture student. In 1957 they were married, and the former Chloe Wofford now became Toni Morrison. The marriage, however, didn't last. It ended in 1965, leaving Morrison with the prospect of raising two children. When they separated, Morrison was still pregnant with her second child. Depressed, but still guided by the inner strengths taught by her family, she resigned her teaching position and returned briefly to Lorain for the birth of her second son. From there she went to Syracuse, New York, where she had landed an editing job with I. W. Singer Publishing House, a subsidiary of Random House. Within two years, she moved from editing text books to editing trade books, and by 1967 she became a Senior Editor at Random House in New York City. From this position, she helped to lead an awakening of black culture in America, encouraging the publication of such writers as Toni Cade Bambara and Gayle Jones.

Meanwhile, Morrison decided to try her own hand at writing a novel. But as a divorced single woman raising two children in addition to holding down a job, sometimes two, she was forced to write in fits and starts, during stolen moments from work and family responsibilities. "I wrote," she recalls, "like someone with a dirty habit. Secretly, compulsively, slyly."[8] To begin with, she told herself that she was writing the novel, which was an expansion of her earlier story about the little black girl who dreamed of blue eyes, only for herself. And she told herself that she didn't really care if it was published or not. But after she finally finished the manuscript, she had to admit great disappointment when publisher after publisher turned it down. Finally, it was accepted by Holt, Rinehart, and Winston, and published with the title *The Bluest Eye*.

Even before its publication, Morrison began working on her second novel. She had found her life's obsession. When *Sula* came out in 1974, it was clear to everybody that *The Bluest Eye* had indeed been the work of an important new talent. Aside from receiving very favorable reviews, *Sula* was nominated for a National Book Award. Also appearing in 1974 was *The Black Book*, a "scrapbook" covering 300 years of African-American life. While she edited this project, Morrison became especially interested in researching the history of the slave narratives. Among the many slave stories she came across was the heroic journey of

Margaret Garner, an escaped Kentucky slave who in 1850 attempted to kill her children rather than see them enslaved. So taken was Morrison by this story that several years later it became the seed for *Beloved*, her fifth novel.

Morrison added yet another job to her busy life as mother, editor, and writer when she accepted a lectureship at Yale University to teach creative writing and African-American literature. If one wondered what she did for fun, if she ever had a free moment, she was bound to give the following answer: "I don't do any of the so-called fun things in life. Writing is what I do, for me that is where it is—where the vacation is, the fun is, the danger, the excitement—all of that is in my work."[9] Fortunately, she found more time for "fun," for her work, after 1977. That year she resigned her teaching position, since her third novel made her family's financial situation much more secure. When *Song of Solomon* came out, it was greeted with a great deal of enthusiasm, both by the reading public and the critics. The first black novel since Richard Wright's *Native Son* to be selected by the Book-of-the-Month Club as a primary offering, it became a best seller. Then it won the National Book Critics Circle Award plus the American Academy and Institute of Arts and Letters Award. Further recognition came when President Jimmy Carter appointed Morrison to the National Council on the Arts.

With her success came many invitations to speak and some attractive offers to teach. Though busier than ever, she still had teaching in her blood, and so she accepted positions as an associate professor at SUNY Purchase and at Bard College in New York. All the while, she was working on her fourth novel. When *Tar Baby* was published in 1981, it became a best-seller and brought Morrison even wider attention. *Newsweek* magazine ran a cover story on her, celebrating the wealth of her fiction. With all this good fortune coming her way, Morrison finally felt free to resign her editing position at Random House in 1984. Helping her make this reluctant decision was an offer by the State University of New York at Albany to become the Albert Schweitzer Professor of Humanities. While at Albany, she wrote her first play. *Dreaming Emmett*, which focused on a young lynching victim, was produced in 1985.

Looking back, it is not surprising that Morrison would try her hand at play writing. Her sense of drama, her impeccable ear for dialogue, and her visual sense are virtues found in all her novels. These virtues, along with others that she developed over the years, are especially evident in *Beloved*, her recent and most praised novel. When *Beloved* was published in 1987, it became a best-seller like Morrison's previous two novels. The next year it was awarded the Pulitzer Prize for fiction. This prize only helped to confirm the obvious, that Morrison had arrived as a major novelist. Subsequently, she was offered and accepted the Robert F. Goheen Professorship in the Humanities at Princeton University, where she remains at the present while continuing work on a trilogy of novels that began with *Beloved*. In the spring of 1992 *Jazz* came out, the second volume of this trilogy that Morrison hopes will crown her career.

* * * * * * * *

In 1990 the Museum of African-American History in Detroit mounted a photographic exhibition of this country's leading black women. Asked what she thought of being selected as one of the honored persons, Morrison responded with mixed feelings. She had to admit that she was flattered, but she had reservations about being held up as a kind of role model for young black women. For one thing, she was disturbed by the implication that somehow black people have a greater need than others for idealized leaders. And she was uncomfortable with the perceived notion that she was a kind of sage whose writing offered the final solution to life's questions. That was not how she saw herself as a writer. "You write, not because you have the answers . . . because you don't," she said. "The only answer you really have is the work you do."[10]

For a full understanding of what Morrison's work ultimately says, it's useful to consider how she goes about saying it, beginning with a look at the actual process of her writing. The process is first emotionally inspired, then intellectually controlled. Before she begins a new novel, Morrison ruminates about its subject matter and style at great length. During this incubation period, she might make notes to herself or write down various comments on her sense of the evolving story. Sometimes she writes out a loose precis. Never an outline though. Once a book starts forming in her mind, she thinks about it constantly. But however great the mental compulsion, she is careful not to rush the moment when she actually begins the composition. "I may think about it for two years," she says, "before I even get down to shaping a sentence on a page."[11] Significantly enough, that "shaped" sentence is likely to be the *last* sentence that will appear in the finished new novel. Never does it turn out to be the first. Morrison believes that "the beginnings can stop you, if you don't have them right." So, she adds, "I just *start!*" Once she starts, she begins accumulating scenes she has worked out to her satisfaction. Always, she strives in these scenes for "the feeling, the language, the metaphor" that was signaled by the first "shaped" sentence she put down.[12] Of course, writing in such a fragmentary way runs the risk that some scenes might not fit into the final scheme. But in Morrison's case, that hardly ever happens, because she uses this crystallization as a constant guide; and because she knows she will in any event spend a great deal of time revising and polishing her work, she feels free to try out all sorts of approaches as she goes along. The result is a style of writing distinguished by an unusual mix of imaginative range and decided authority.

Critics are naturally tempted to provide labels for a writer's individual style. In Morrison's case, the temptation has been especially great. But the attempt to find such a label has been generally unsatisfactory, even at times confusing. The apparent problem has been that, paradoxically, while Morrison is recognized on one hand as writing like no other novelist, on the other hand there is the critical tendency to draw overly strict comparisons between her way of writing and other traditions or fashions. Thus, she has sometimes been called a magical realist, sometimes a mythical symbolist. Her writing has been allied with the conventions of fabulism and folklore. Enthusiasts of the grotesque aspects in her writing have seen her as a kind of black gothicist. More traditional critics have described her as a kind of black classicist. And so on. Of course, all of these labels have an application to Morrison's style, but only in a limited way. In the end, Morrison simply defies such categorization because her general style is made up of the specific necessities of the narrative at hand.

Shining through this stylistic mix is Morrison's fundamental concern with language itself. When asked at one point what she thought distinguished her fiction, she answered: "The language, only the language."[13] One could argue with this limiting self-assessment, but not with the implied suggestion that the most striking quality about her writing is the language. Specifically, the "black" language of her people. In using this language, Morrison identifies with "the thing that black people love so

much—the saying of words, holding them on the tongue, experimenting with them, playing with them." In her passion for
language that can "suggest and be provocative at the same time,"
Morrison believes she may resemble the black sermonizers who
can "make you stand up out of your seat, make you love yourself
and hear yourself."[14] Actually, though, it's more accurate to
compare her to a poet than a sermonizer. Morrison herself has
resisted being described as a kind of poet. She believes that when
her style is called "poetic," there is a tendency to take the word as
connoting ornamental, luxuriating richness of language that is
self-consciously literary. Those connotations would certainly be
misleading. But if the word "poetic" is taken to mean that she
has a poet's sense of using pure language, then the term surely
applies. She has indicated as much herself. When prompted to
comment on her craft and what inspired it, she has said she
"wanted to restore the language that black people spoke to its
original power."[15] With this goal in mind, she deliberately set
out "to clean the language and give words back their original
meanings, not the one that's sabotaged by constant use." She has
discovered that "if you work very carefully, you can clean up ordinary words and repolish them, make parabolic language seem
alive again."[16]

At the same time, Morrison has said she wants her language to do "what music used to do" for black people in America. What music used to do was to provide the primary means
to sustaining a unique culture. This culture, based on the idea of
a consciously shared community, is now threatened with disappearance, Morrison believes. Black Americans used to live
mostly in actual or abstracted villages, compounds, or enclaves.
These communities expressed their unique character and unifying beliefs and aspirations through various means of communication, usually coded against intrusion from the threatening
white world. Of these means of communication, music was the
most essential. But in the commercially driven media world
that now exists, cultural distinctions are constantly lost to the as-
similating process of popular fashions. New generations of
blacks are progressively more educated, but also more ignorant
of their unique traditions. Their knowledge of black music may
not extend beyond their record collection. This is where Morrison wishes to step in. She can't "save" black communal music.
But she can, and does, aspire to keep this tradition alive by making room for it in her narratives, and by purposely employing its

principles as an integrating feature of her style.

Morrison deliberately accompanies her narratives with what might be called a sound track of black music. When faced with intense experiences of happiness or pain, her characters often break into folk songs, gospel numbers, popular tunes, the blues, or they simply whistle or hum. These musical moments or interludes are in turn characteristically allied with various images placed in the texts as reflective reminders of the communal values and inspirations black music was designed to express. Elevating the text as a whole is the special sound of Morrison's language. This sound may best be described as "literary jazz."[17] Morrison herself has said she is always attempting to write in "a black style" that, for clarification, could be compared to what black musicians try to do.[18] More precisely, she is thinking of black jazz musicians, whose music is marked by expressive range, rhythmic patterns, spontaneity, and intimacy. These general qualities Morrison adapts to her writing, along with some more specific features that are jazz-like. Thus, her novels can generally be said to open with a sounded motif, which is then repeated and re-sounded in a circular and reverberating way, building to recognizably dominant themes. Purposely complicating the developing patterns are events of inversion, juxtaposition, dissonance, and surprising variations or modulations of the opening motif. All these factors, though, are in the end organized harmoniously by an aspiring lead instrument, or the narrative voice, in Morrison's case.

One other special quality found in black jazz that Morrison aspires to is its elliptical, open-ended nature. Unlike classical music, for example, jazz doesn't attempt to provide a formally enclosed kind of satisfaction. Instead, it suggests something purposely left out or referred to incompletely. This kind of music agitates and offers emotional, responsive freedom. There is form and structure, to be sure, just as there are various leading chords, but in the end there is no insistence on one shape, and there is no clearly final chord. Something else is promised; but that something else has to be discovered by the audience in the music's evocative resonance. Morrison wishes her novels to work in a similar fashion. She wants to create "that feeling of something held in reserve and the sense that there is more—that you can't have it all right now."[19]

While applying this stylistic strategy throughout the course of her stories, Morrison says she finds herself "fretting" especially hard over finding and developing a sound that, although artistically wrought for appropriate suggestiveness, seems natural and spontaneous. Morrison has a wonderful ear for the music of language, and this is the main reason why she is so successful in realizing the sound she desires. But at the same time, she knows a stylistic trick or two that can work to her advantage. She deliberately avoids using adverbs, particularly when describing how somebody says something in the context of a dialogue. When she first writes down the vocabulary for her characters, she often finds herself using the print-quality of language. But then she rewrites it systematically to recapture the original oral quality, putting in the nuances, intonations, gestures, and volumes that reflect not only the *heard* language of general experience but also the distinct, particular language each character would be bound to use. Finally, she consciously pares the dialogue down, first to the essential words, then to their appropriate textual sounds "so that the reader has to hear it."[20]

Obviously, then, Morrison depends on her readers to be highly participatory. From this readership, Morrison certainly hopes for a clear intellectual response. But she says she also wants "a very strong visceral and emotional response" similar to the one a jazz player hopes for, perhaps even more precisely similar to the one a black preacher ultimately inspires in a responsive congregation. In such a responsive relationship, the congregation not only listens but also takes part in the sermon: approving, disapproving, interjecting, or otherwise echoing the words of the preacher. Ideally, for Morrison, the readers of her novels become so involved in the process they will have a sense "that it is not I who do it, it is they who do."[21]

If any of this appears to be self-consciously experimental in style, that would be a misunderstanding of Morrison's basic approach. Actually, she is trying to go *back* to a particular tradition that only seems new because it has almost died out in the culture of black Americans. This is the tradition of African story telling which centered around the griot. Thus, Morrison says, she is "simply trying to re-create something out of an old form . . . the something that defines what makes a book 'black.'"[22] In the tradition of the griot, the central idea was to create oral stories with an open-ended quality. The expectation was that as the stories were told and retold, they would take on newly imagined lives, again and again. Morrison experienced some of this kind of story-telling while she was growing up. When she finally decided to become a story teller herself, she looked back and decided she must try to be a kind of literary griot, because of her conviction that in this way she might succeed in realizing through the written word what the oral story tellers used to do for their listeners—providing them with a kind of cultural "life support system."[23]

From this angle, Morrison tries to write novels that give the impression of having come from people who aren't writers. She wants it to appear as though no author tells the story. The narratives simply start and go on, apparently without a definite structure, unfolding and meandering in various directions all at once, it seems. This approach may on the surface sound chaotic, but of course it isn't. Holding everything together is a guiding voice. This voice, however, although heard throughout the narrative, is not easily identified because Morrison avoids using a simple and personally authoritative point-of-view. She tries to create an illusion that the point-of-view belongs to the multiple characters. In fact, it belongs to a narrator who is always present but never admits to the reader the role being played. This voice doesn't have a personality as such. It can only be defined by its sound. That voice can be trusted, however, because it has a comfortable and intimate quality, the kind that invites the reader to identify with it. Like the reader, this voice can be deeply affected, or even surprised, by the narrative events. In other words, this is a voice that is always involved, even if sometimes it is forced to abandon itself, such as when it wants us to hear the interior dialogues of characters. But it always wants to remain invisible. In a directly technical sense, Morrison is obviously the narrator, and it is her personal voice that slides "in" and "out" of her various characters. When she is "out," however, the reader doesn't suddenly discover a narrative authority commenting on or pointing to the text. The story continues as if it were just *told* by no one in particular.[24]

Morrison's work has often been compared to William Faulkner's, mainly because of the "oral" quality of both writers. Another point of comparison can be found in the fact that they both specialize in what Morrison calls "village literature," where the focus is on a particular people and their isolated place. In Morrison's case, of course, the focus is on the black people who live in communities that haven't yet been swallowed up by urban sprawl. These are the types of people that Morrison knew when she grew up in her hometown. But it should be emphasized that Morrison's fiction is not autobiographical. She goes back to her formative memories only for initial inspiration. Then she frees her imagination to create communities reflecting as fully as possible the essential experience of her "tribe."[25] Her success in creating such communities is often brilliant in the specificity of place. When asked to explain her strong sense of place, Morrison has ventured to guess that it might simply come from a natural knack women have, since their usual situation is to be tied to a room, a house, or some particular place. More likely, her special sense of place comes from a dramatic and imaginative gift for visualizing, in a specific and at the same time metaphorical way. Indirectly, she has confirmed this conclusion when noting that sometimes her writing can't move along despite the fact she is sure of the action and the dialogue. What she then needs for an impetus is "the scene, the metaphor to begin with. Once I can see the scene, it all happens."[26]

In these scenes, the details are all present, down to such specifics as the colors and numbers of the houses, the finest shades and shadows of daily existence. Needless to say, the characters are also specified with careful observation. This is not only as it should be, but *must* be, in Morrison's fiction. Her characters are all meant to be taken as distinct and complex individuals. None is all good or bad, or only this or that. They embody combinations Morrison takes pains to represent. Often their complexity is increased by Morrison's tendency to pair characters for reflective effect. Whatever their final make-up, Morrison tries to create her characters in such a way that the reader can see how they are perceived in their world and how at the same times these characters see things through their own eyes. To accomplish this, Morrison doesn't exactly identify with them. More precisely, she does what actors do in their work by attempting to become her characters in a limited way so that she can imagine what they would be likely to focus on and how they would express themselves. Thus Morrison insists that each of her characters must speak "his or her own language, has an individual set of metaphors, and notices certain things differently from other people."[27] Whatever they are like, she says she always loves them all. But the characters she obviously cares for most are two prominently recurring types. The first is the type around whom Morrison usually gathers her story. This is the kind of character who undergoes a process of becoming, of maturing, of finally reaching the point of necessary self-realization or self-discovery. The other type is less traditional, in fact quite radical. These characters Morrison likes to call "the dangerous free people" or "the salt tasters." They are so important to her, and so often misunderstood because of their controversial nature, that Morrison's description of them bears quoting at length: "The salt tasters . . . express either an effort of the will or a freedom of the will. It's all about choosing. Though granted there's an enormous amount of stuff one cannot chose. But if you own yourself, you can make some types of choices, take certain kinds of risks. They do, and they're misunderstood. They are the misunderstood people in the world. There's a wildness that they have, a nice wildness. It has bad effects in society such as the one in which we live. It's pre-Christ in the best sense. It's Eve. When I see this wildness gone in a person, it's sad. This special lack of restraint, which is a part of human life and is best typified in certain black males, is of particular interest to me. It's in black men despite the reasons society says they're not supposed to have it. Everybody knows who 'that man' is, and they may give him bad names and call him a 'street nigger'; but when you take away the vocabulary of denigration, what you have is somebody who is fearless and who is comfortable with that fearlessness. It's not about meanness. It's a kind of self-flagellant resistance to certain kinds of control, which is fascinating. Opposed to accepted notions of progress, the lock-step life, they live in the world unreconstructed."[28]

Whatever else might be said about Morrison's central characters, they all move in the direction of tragedy. At the end of her narratives, underlying the typical ambiguity, is an assured sense of the seriousness of life. Things don't promise to simply fall apart, but there is a climactic emphasis on the enduring chill of human suffering. The most comforting note is that there has been a catharsis and a revelation of the shared condition of existence. The least comforting is the promise that while the anxiety of human pain remains, there is an attending loss of innocence. Morrison's endings seem to suggest that the loss of the belief in human innocence is a necessary step toward redemption, and that suffering precedes the essential knowledge that must be acquired. What is this essential knowledge Morrison points to? To say the knowledge found in Greek tragedies would certainly not be off the mark. The primary influence on Morrison's vision, just as on her style, is always that of her heritage. As she herself suspects, however, her tragic mode, particularly as it is expressed in her endings, has been at least partially influenced by her formal education and training in the classics while at college.[29]

Again, like Greek tragedies, Morrison's stories tend to have fairly simple outlines but are populated by complicated characters. These characters have layers of simplicity and mystery, of good and evil. In the final analysis, the central characters also embody issues and ideas important to Morrison. For Morrison, writing stories that are not about intellectual questions holds no interest. In fact, she says her stories and characters occur to her initially in the shape of ideas. It should be noted, however, that these ideas are usually "old," in the sense that they have been worried over by thinkers and writers for countless years. Morrison honestly describes them as "cliches." She adds, however, that "a cliche is a cliche because it's worthwhile," and if it hasn't yet been discarded, the reason is that "a good cliche can never be overwritten; it's still a mystery."[30] Thus, for example, Morrison points to the concepts surrounding such issues as beauty and ugliness, or love and death. Although these concepts are anything but fresh, they continue to be mysterious, and many people still worry over them and write about them. In writing about such "old" ideas, Morrison says she tries "to get underneath them and see what they mean, and understand the impact they have had on what people do." Going on, she says she can certainly imagine failing in various ways when she writes; but whatever may go wrong, she will at least always know she will have tried to make her stories "about something that is important to me, and the subjects that are important in the world are the same ones that have always been important."[31]

One subject or theme continually prominent in literature, particularly American literature, is the problem of survival. After they finish, Morrison wants her readers to think about who survived the strains and stresses of the story's tensions, and why. Although she tries hard not to be didactic, and avoids editorializing at all cost, she at the same time hopes to present stories that provide lessons in getting through the various danger zones of personal and social life without losing one's heart. She hopes the course for her characters leads in the end to moral security. Her characters aren't literary puppets, however, and might not make it all the way to such a haven. At the end, they might wind up in a trap. They, in fact, often find themselves in this position because Morrison is deeply interested in "the complexity of how people behave under duress . . . the qualities they show at the end of an event when their backs are against the wall."[32] Whatever the ultimate destiny of these characters, Morrison doesn't have them bow out with simple answers to the difficult questions of being human. She knows there aren't any such answers.

Like the theme of survival, the theme of self-discovery is very prominent in American literature. And so it also is in Morrison's work. In fact, it can be argued that self-discovery turns out to be her overriding theme. When asked about what her basic themes were, Morrison has mentioned love and freedom in addition to that of survival. If one takes all her writing into account, however, it becomes apparent that even though she doesn't specify it as such, her grand theme is actually that of self-discovery, or its close variation, the issue of self-definition. Again and again, Morrison creates central characters lost in some way, characters who are trying, or at least characters who should try, to find their way toward a fuller appreciation of the world in which they move and a fuller understanding of themselves as both involved participants and private human beings. After one grasps the fact that this is indeed Morrison's over-arching concern, then one has as good a key to her writing as a whole as there is. No other single critical approach works as well. Many others have been tried. A survey of the books and articles written about Morrison's work clearly indicates that she is perceived to be one of the most elusive of our contemporary writers, so many different critical approaches have been tried. Just to name a few, there are the systematic approaches used by existential, feminist, Romantic, archetypal, or Marxist believers. None of these readings, nor that of any other fashionable critical system, works quite satisfactorily in the end. They all seem tortured and strained in their logic. The fact turns out to be that Morrison (i.e. Morrison's work) is both too complicated and too simple for a rigid critical methodology. Just like human beings, particularly human beings still in the process of discovering themselves.

Morrison's characters usually discover they must go back to their African heritage if they are to find themselves in the fullest sense. However, they may find other useful ways as well during the process. Which is to say that Morrison doesn't simply preach that a return to original roots is a panacea for black Americans. She is often misunderstood in this regard because she is credited by a number of critics with deliberately writing

about her people's experiences from an African perspective. To
some extent, these critics are right. Morrison often draws on
African myths, folklore, and popular wisdom, with many of her
characters showing they are directly or indirectly influenced by
these sources. At the same time, however, Morrison is also
prone to work Western myths and folklore into her texts, as well
as classic fairy tales, fables, and nursery rhymes. The fact is that
Morrison is eclectic in her use of sources and influences. She
will use whatever works, and fuse the parts into a whole. What
she understands is that human truth resides in competing
myths and stories, and that personal actions and cultural behavior are affected by these multiple tensions. The thing that inter-
ests her most in this area is how these tensions work on a sub-
conscious level in African-Americans. Thus she tends to focus
on their dreams and imaginings, their collective legends and
rituals, because she believes that together these phenomena reveal their characters most fully and best answer what one critic
has called "the ubiquitous question: What makes black folk act
that way?"[33] The answer lies to a great extent in their African
roots; but Morrison also shows there are other influential
sources which should be taken into account.

   Because her most recent novels emphasize the history of
blacks systematically victimized by whites, some critics have decided that Morrison has taken a turn toward political writing.
The fact is that politics is not a new aspect in her novels. Politics
just plays a more obvious role in *Beloved* and *Jazz* because of
their subject matter and the nature of the stories. In earlier novels, Morrison would argue that she is also political, if less obviously so. "The work must be political," she has said. "It must
have that as its thrust. That's a pejorative term in critical circles
now: if a work of art has any political influence in it, somehow
it's tainted. My feeling is just the opposite: if it has none it is
tainted . . . The best art is political and you ought to be able to
make it unquestionably political and irrevocably beautiful at the
same time."[34]

   Morrison is especially concerned with sexual politics as
they affect black women. She continuously shows how sexist
behavior, both in and out of the bounds of the black community,
can be an oppressive force. Significantly, though, she avoids trying to present some kind of revolutionary solution, and never
slides into polemics on the subject. Her role, as she sees it, is instead to celebrate the unique culture black women have man-

aged to develop in the hostile environment of white America. In her youth she learned to respond to the strong women who somehow retained the traditional values and folk arts of their original culture; and in her maturity she has felt the obligation to sustain at least their memory. In fact, she has come to feel this obligation with the intensity of a calling. That is why, when asked to describe what she thought she was trying to do more than anything in her novels, she gave the following summarizing answer: "My attempt, although I never say any of this, until I'm done, is to deal with something that is nagging me, but, when I think about it in a large sense, I use the phrase 'bear witness' to explain what my work is for. I have this creepy sensation . . . something is about to be lost and will never be retrieved. . . . Our past . . . if we women, if we black women, if we Third-World women in America don't know it, then, it is not known to anybody at all   . . . And somebody has to tell." [35]

Chapter 2

The Bluest Eye

Toni Morrison has been a consistently insightful and helpful critic of her work. With regard to her first novel, she has indicated that her plan was to take love and the effects of its scarcity in the world as her major themes,[1] concentrating on the interior lives of her characters, especially those of an enclosed community.[2] Her stated aim is to show "how to survive *whole* in a world where we are all of us, in some measure, *victims of something*."[3] Morrison's broad vision extends beyond the individual to one that explores self-discovery in relation to a "shared history."[4] In a film interview, Morrison has stated, "I suppose *The Bluest Eye* is about one's dependency on the world for identification, self-value, feelings of worth."[5] In order to dramatize the destructive effects of this kind of dependency, she intentionally exaggerates to find the limits.

Morrison's rich novels of growing awareness, personal survival, and individual responsibility are often misunderstood or given limited interpretations when readers fail to pay close attention to her use of multiple narrative perspectives.[6] These shifts from first to third, intimate to omniscient, guide readers through often harrowing personal experiences and give personal as well as lyrical overviews. In *The Bluest Eye*, Claudia MacTeer provides a child's point of view—sometimes from an adult perspective—while an omniscient voice relates information unknown by Claudia. There are also passages shifting between third person omniscient and first person stream of consciousness. Morrison uses these combined voices to give varied perspectives without resorting to authorial intrusion or preaching. She wants her readers to participate fully in her fiction, to go with her to examine the often painful circumstances of her characters' lives.[7]

Survival, a theme running throughout Morrison's fiction, is difficult for the strongest of her characters. For eleven year old Pecola Breedlove, the focal character of *The Bluest Eye*, discovering a means to affirm her own identity is thwarted at every turn. Morrison's first novel takes place in 1941, when Pecola, an innocent and convenient victim of her community's frustration, anger, ignorance, and shame, becomes a woman. Raped by her father, she gives birth to a stillborn child and then escapes her sense of ugliness into madness, convinced that she has magically been given blue eyes.

Morrison's title, like her point of view, has multiple significance. Most obviously, the title refers to Pecola's only desire in life: to have the bluest eyes. These, she believes, will reverse the bleak circumstances of her life, making her pretty and thus valued by others. Teachers will smile, children will cease their taunts, shopkeepers will be helpful, her parents will show affection. But Morrison is also punning on the title's suggestive possibilities, indicating the "gloomy ego" of Pecola.[8] The title also relates to Claudia MacTeer, who dismembers her despised white baby dolls, trying to discover the secret of their loveability. "Blue," in this case, doesn't simply mean "gloomy"; it suggests the blues, those sweetly sad songs of loss and reconciliation sung by Claudia's mother and Miss Marie in this novel.[9] And the "eye," or "I," refers specifically to Claudia and the effect of Pecola's story on her "seeing" and understanding.

Claudia's story of loss and reconciliation assumes the form of a pastoral elegy. There is the formal evocation, a brief remembrance linking Pecola's stillborn child with Nature's failure to reproduce in 1941; an eloquent expression of grief, the main body of the novel entailing conscious and unconscious acts of cruelty leading to Pecola's insanity; and the consolation, Claudia's discovery through expression. As Claudia begins Pecola's story, she says, "There is really nothing more to say except why. But since *why* is difficult to handle, one must take refuge in how."[10] When Claudia ends her recollection, however, readers have insight into the *why*, which is Morrison's aim all along.

As narrator, nine year old Claudia stands on the periphery of most of the story's action, an ingenuous yet perceptive observer whose own innocence erodes less violently but no less surely than Pecola's. Though Claudia's point of view is limited, she nevertheless experiences all she needs to, largely because of caste and class. The MacTeers live in a drafty house, scavenge coal during winter, eat an abundance of turnip greens, and look forward to spring, when life seems easier. Despite the MacTeers' struggle, they are far better off than the Breedloves because the MacTeers own their property, forge a stable family relationship, and maintain solidarity with their neighbors. Above all, as their name suggests, the MacTeers have sympathy. Their generosity leads them to shelter Pecola when Cholly Breedlove sets fire to his rented property and puts his family "outdoors."

Once Claudia and her sister Frieda discover how complaisant Pecola is, they widen their sympathy to friendship. Indeed, theirs is the only friendship Pecola ever enjoys because Claudia and Frieda never assume superiority. The children share much in common: gender, age, race, poverty, ignorance, guilt, and awareness of adult anger—most of which they cannot control. Despite her identification with Pecola, Claudia senses a fundamental difference. While Pecola can see only her parents' anger, Claudia is confident of love "Thick and rich as Alaga syrup" behind her mother's outbursts (14). Ironically, the culminating token of this parental affection occurs at Christmas in the form of a big, blue-eyed babydoll. Realizing the gift is given out of love, Claudia nevertheless "was physically revolted by and secretly frightened by those round moronic eyes, the pancake face, and orangeworm hair" (20). Instead of cherishing the doll, Claudia takes it apart, trying to discover the source of its desirability. In destroying the doll, Claudia asserts her own value, for the doll, reflecting a white ideal of beauty, is inimical to Claudia's sense of self. She recognizes—as the adults do not—that if the doll is perceived to be pretty, then she is not.

This pervasive *white* standard of beauty adopted by so many characters in *The Bluest Eye* is at the heart of the cruelty and destruction that occurs because it fails to recognize and value difference. Indeed, this single standard wholly denies difference by ignoring the obvious fact that it exists. Much of the impetus to conform to a white ideal is engendered by the movies, where the physical appearance of white stars such as Jean Harlow, Betty Grable, and Shirley Temple becomes inextricable from their enviable, luxurious screen lives, particularly when compared to the few stereotyped black characters featured in the films of the 1930's and 40s. Like many, Pauline Breedlove is seduced by the movies. Pregnant and lonely, she finds comfort in the theaters, where she is deeply influenced by "the most destructive ideas in the history of human thought," romantic love and physical beauty (97). As so often happens in the movies, beauty becomes confused with virtue, and Pauline, accepting this, gathers "self-contempt by the heap" (97). She becomes an exacting judge, automatically rating people in terms of physical beauty. But when she is forced to rank herself at the bottom of her scale after losing a front tooth (appropriately at the movies and with her hair arranged like Jean Harlow's), Pauline orchestrates a substitute life as the Fishers' "ideal servant." In their home she has "beauty, order, praise" and a surrogate daughter who looks like Shirley Temple (101). Pauline fails to recognize what she abandons for this daily illusion.

The sacrifice, as Morrison makes clear throughout her work, is the essential self, the whole.[11] For in conforming to a role defined by others, and in confusing self with role, Pauline denies any possibility of growth. And here we see her representing many who, in adopting white values and standards of behavior, deny their essential value, substituting false—even destructive—standards. This adoption, or "adjustment without improvement," as Claudia describes her own defection, brings about varying degrees of damage (22).

Two of the most extreme representatives of such damage occur in the "Winter" section of *The Bluest Eye*. The first is light skinned Maureen Peal, whose relative affluence and popularity prove the advantages of being nearly white. Like Pauline, Maureen has been partially educated by the movies. She instantly recognizes Pecola's name as that of the "pretty," nearly white girl in *Imitation of Life* who "hates her mother 'cause she is black and ugly" (57). As her comment reveals, Maureen has fully internalized traditional white associations of darkness with ugliness. But darkness also becomes associated in her mind (as in the dominant community) with sexuality. Eager to pursue the "truth" of the boys' taunts concerning Cholly Breedlove's sexuality ("Black e mo Black e mo Ya daddy sleeps nekked"), Maureen momentarily befriends Pecola one afternoon after Frieda rescues her from the boys (55). Shortly thereafter, when Pecola denies having seen her naked father, Maureen turns on her, affirming the taunt and going still further: "I am cute and you ugly. Black and ugly black e mos" (61). Her attack, directed at all three girls, hits home. Claudia dwells on the apparent truth of her statement, thinking that "If she was cute—and if anything

could be believed, she was—then we were not. And what did
that mean? We were lesser" (61). She also recognizes that the
source of this conviction isn't Maureen. "The *Thing* to fear,"
she concludes, "was the *Thing* that made *her* beautiful, and not
us" (62).

An even more extreme version of Maureen occurs in
Geraldine, whose internalization of white standards creates hatred and violence. Typical of one kind of middle class female,
Geraldine is taught "thrift, patience, high morals, and good
manners. In short how to get rid of the funkiness of passion, the
funkiness of nature. The funkiness of the wide range of human
emotions" (68). By conforming her beliefs and behavior to a narrow standard instead of developing her own, Geraldine remains
emotionally hollow, unable to feel affection for any living thing,
except, perhaps, a cat. This character's unimaginative devotion
to neatness and correct white behavior inevitably creates a mon-
ster, Louis Junior, whose nature is so deprived of normal expression that his primary pleasure is terrorizing his mother's cat.
Appropriately, his feline victim is black with blue eyes, signifying Junior's antipathy toward black and white worlds.
(Forbidden to play with dark-skinned children, Junior is generally ostracized by whites.) Confusing play with distraction, one
afternoon Junior draws Pecola and the cat together in a scheme
of victimization. Luring Pecola into his house with the promise
of showing her kittens, Junior throws the cat in her face. Later,
he swings the cat by its leg and flings it into the radiator. When
Geraldine walks into the room, Junior blames Pecola. A glance
at poor, unkempt Pecola tells Geraldine everything; she believes
her son. Worse, she fails to see a child; she sees a type, a class
representative for whom she has only disgust:

> They were everywhere. They slept six in a bed. . . .
> Grass wouldn't grow where they lived. Flowers died
> Shades fell down. Tin cans and tires blossomed where
> they lived. . . . Like flies they hovered; like flies they
> settled (75).

Her horror of contamination prompts a devastating outburst
echoing Maureen's linkage of sexuality to darkness: "Get out . . .
You nasty little black bitch" (75). Once more an outcast because
of color, Pecola absorbs its lesson.

Rejection by the more affluent segments of society is bad
enough, but Pecola is cast out by her own family. *The Bluest Eye*

opens with Claudia's account of how Pecola came to stay with her after Cholly Breedlove, in a drunken rage, put his family "outdoors" by burning down their rented quarters (17). The distinction between "outdoors" and "out" has considerable significance since the former is "the end of something, an irrevocable, physical fact" while the latter is something over which one has no control (18). The black community is outraged by Cholly's act, a conscious blow at his family's tenuous unity. However, we, as readers, are given details which should inform our perspective of Cholly's act.

Salvaged from a junk heap by his Great Aunt Jimmy when only four days old, Cholly Breedlove has grown up with scarce emotional resources. The strongest personal link of his childhood is forged with Blue Jack, an alcoholic drayman who entertains Cholly and gives him some sense of self by relating local history and sharing thoughts about life. But Cholly's relationship with Blue is short lived when Aunt Jimmy dies. First, Cholly's self-image is damaged after he is humiliated by leering white voyeurs during his sexual initiation, and then Cholly is denied by his own father. An omniscient narrator relates the agonizing circumstances of Cholly's sexual humiliation, noting that Cholly directs his anger at his partner, Darlene, not because he believes her to be the source of his humiliation (directing his anger at the white men would be deadly) but because he wasn't able to protect her. Cholly's anger soon turns to fear that Darlene is pregnant, and he flees in the only direction he believes he will find understanding—toward a father he has never seen. Samson Fuller, however, seems more interested in dice than in a fourteen year old boy.

Morrison indicates the profound injury his father's lack of interest inflicts on Cholly through Cholly's immediate withdrawal to infantilism, first as he soils himself and soon after when he draws himself into a fetal position under a river pier. A reborn Cholly emerges from the river, who becomes "dangerously free" because he lacks the emotional resources to give coherence to the pain as well as the few pleasures of his life: "He was alone with his own perceptions and appetites, and they alone interested him" (125-126). Cholly's marriage to Pauline completes the process of emotional isolation when he discovers that "Nothing, nothing interested him now" (126). And fatherhood shoves Cholly from the brink of indifference into dysfunction since he has neither models nor expectations. He acts solely on momentary whim.

The Bluest Eye begins with Cholly's putting Pecola outdoors; it climaxes with his completing the process in the most
final way short of murder. He rapes Pecola, wanting at first "to
be tender" but soon discovering that "the tenderness would not
hold" (128). Pecola's only response to her father's act is the
"hollow suck of air in the back of her throat. Like the rapid loss
of air from a circus balloon," suggesting the vacuum Cholly
leaves behind (128).

Though Cholly is responsible for his actions, he merely
serves as the instrument of a culture which values females primarily for their beauty and then assesses their worth according
to narrow racist standards. Cholly's "act," as it were, has gone on
long before and continues after his actions. At least, as Claudia
observes, he wanted to touch his daughter. Pauline Breedlove
responds to the rape by beating Pecola, an act not much less brutal than Cholly's. There nevertheless seem to be extenuating
circumstances to illustrate the *why* instead of the *how*.

Like her husband, Pauline lacks emotional ties. It may be
argued that this is the direct result of her physical and thus emotional displacement in her move from South to North.[12] But
Morrison makes very clear Pauline's sense of emotional es-
trangement has actually been life long. As a child growing up in
a large Alabama family, Pauline feels "she had never felt at
home anywhere or that she belonged any place" (88). She coun-
terbalances her sense of isolation by arranging items, especially
domestic items. After her marriage and move to Lorain, Pauline
experiences increasing loneliness. Her substitution of movies—
and Hollywood images of beauty and love—estranges Pauline,
not just from others but from her fragile sense of self. After this,
Pauline can "display the style and imagination of what she believed to be her own true self" only during her fights with
Cholly (36). With her children, she is less physically brutal, but
no less emotionally violent.

Paradoxically, her children are the very reason for her
choices. Because of them, Pauline sees the need to give coherence to her life. Especially after becoming the Fishers' "ideal
servant," her choices are dominated by her desire for unifying
and simplifying. In the Fisher home Pauline finds what seems
both pleasing and gratifying to her, the "beauty, order, cleanli-
ness, and praise" absent in her own home (101). However,
rather than share, "Pauline kept this order, this beauty for herself, a private world" (101). Her sense of worth resides in the au-

thority she wields in the Fisher home and the "respectability" she beats into her children "and in so doing [teaches] them fear . . . fear of life" (102). A zealous convert to a Puritan ethic in both her attitude toward work and human sexuality, Pauline finds "All the meaningfulness of her life in her work" (102). She has so fully adopted white expectations that during a key incident in the Fisher kitchen, when Pecola accidentally spills a hot pie on the floor, Pauline fails to see her child's burn, only the ruin of her clean floor. So conditioned are her reflexes—so inverted her perspective—that she strikes Pecola and comforts her white charge.

Both Cholly and Pauline represent miserable failures as parents, and their failures are the consequences of stunted selves unable to discover an imaginative means of transforming experience.[13] Of Cholly, the omniscient narrator relates that the "pieces of [his] life could become coherent only in the head of a musician" (135). And Pauline has "missed—without knowing what she missed—paints and crayons" (89). Without imaginative resources and a discipline of emotional expression other than violence, Cholly lacks a means of striking a balance between the chaos of his reality and a reasonable coherence. Pauline, by contrast, squeezes her life into a narrow coherence, but in so doing, she extinguishes her vitality—significantly embodied in the taste and color she associates with sensual pleasure. The very pleasures which haunt her dream life are denied in favor of sterile fabrications which she then employs as justification for her "moral" behavior. The results, embodied in their daughter, are tragic.

Raised to fear life, Pecola never challenges the cruel realities she confronts, both the implicit racism inherent in the Shirley Temple icons as well as the explicit acts which batter her submissive ego. Instead, like many children, she wishes for transformation. But where most children would wish to change the external—place, circumstance, others—Pecola sees herself as the problem: "If her eyes, those eyes that held the pictures [of her reality] and knew the sights—if those eyes were different . . . she herself would be different" (40). She asks God to grant her blue eyes for a full year before timidly approaching Soaphead Church, a reader and advisor alleged to possess supernatural powers. Though struck by Pecola's request—"Of all the wishes people had brought him—money, love, revenge—this seemed to him the most poignant and the most deserving of fulfillment"—

even Soaphead victimizes her by having her innocently poison a dog he detests (137). But in a grievance letter to God, Soaphead identifies with Pecola as a victim of God's absent mercy. Furthermore, he claims credit for giving Pecola her blue eyes, though he admits only *she* will be able to see them.

Morrison leaves Soaphead's personal responsibility for driving Pecola over the edge of sanity ambiguous, for he is simply another in a long line of victimizers. This character is linked to Pecola in other, equally significant ways, for the elements of Soaphead's background and character are identical with those which have ostracized Pecola throughout her life. Born Elihue Whitcomb of mixed Asian, African, and English blood, Soaphead combines at least three races. Still, he comes from a family convinced that its intellectual superiority stems from its white blood. A lifelong misanthrope, he has only disdain for other people, his arrogance illustrated by his adding "Micah" ("he who is like God") to his name. Soaphead's superior sense of self and contempt for others suppress his most basic urges. This unnatural suppression finally leads him to sexual perversion. Not surprisingly, he is a pedophile, a sometime molester of little girls. Morrison does not fail to inject the distorting influence of religious dogma in Soaphead's background, as his last name, "Church," suggests. There are obvious links connecting his selective religious beliefs to the picture of a white Jesus in Geraldine's house, to the fervor of Pauline's devotion to her church. Represented is not the substance but the appearance of religion, set on an individually selective basis.

Pecola's ultimate fate is to continue living on the fringes of society, a daily reminder of societal culpability as she picks through garbage. Her complete dependency on others for self-identification destroys her, for when society decrees her ugly and therefore unworthy of affection, encouragement, and esteem, Pecola has neither the courage nor the knowledge to argue. She meekly accepts her inferior position because, being so vulnerable, she cannot see other options. But even though Pecola will never discover herself in relation to the world, she is invaluable in helping Claudia come to a greater understanding of herself and her community.

Looking at Pecola, Claudia sees a possible outcome for herself, one that proves the need to struggle. Pecola's unquestioning adoption of a standard which denies her value, which in fact makes her invisible in many cases, is self-destructive.

Without a sense of importance, Pecola cannot counter the antagonistic forces surrounding her. She doesn't retaliate against her taunting schoolmates, she doesn't call Junior a liar, she doesn't return Maureen's insult. In fact, Pecola never makes demands of anyone and is consequently trampled. On the rare occasions when given a preference, Pecola's customary response is, "I don't care" (19). Viewing the consequences, Claudia sees that Pecola needs to care, for if she doesn't, chances are good that no one else will.

Moreover, as Pecola's example remains a disturbing factor in Claudia's memory, she comes to understand the significance of that example to herself and to the community. Claudia sees that Pecola's subservience has made her into a scapegoat.[14] "All of us—all who knew her," she concludes, "felt so wholesome after we cleaned ourselves on her. We were so beautiful when we stood astride her ugliness. Her simplicity decorated us, her guilt sanctified us, her pain made us glow with health, her awkwardness made us think we had a sense of humor" (159). And because Claudia understands how the community has abused Pecola's virtues by taking advantage of them, she also recognizes that the community's goodness is actually hypocrisy: "we were not strong, only aggressive; we were not free, merely licensed; we were not compassionate, we were polite; not good, but well behaved" (159). Most of all, Claudia, through her abiding sense of guilt, learns to feel her responsibility for the fate of another. Despite excuses and her own efforts, she knows that Pecola might have been saved if someone had cared enough to nurture her spirit.

Morrison's vision is not merely limited to the black community, though Pecola clearly represents the social, economic, and political position of African-Americans. More universally, though, Pecola might be seen as the innocent set upon by the world, for Morrison often writes not only about the local human soil but also that "of the entire country," and, in 1941, of the world at war (160). Dealing with the fruit of the soil, she arranges the course of her novel according to the four seasons, beginning with late autumn, when Pecola literally falls from society. During the winter, as already noted, Pecola experiences her darkest season of torture by her schoolmates and abuse by adults. In the spring, she is impregnated, and in the late summer, when marigolds usually flourish, she prematurely gives birth to a dead child.

Morrison's association of marigolds and Pecola's baby is significant in a number of ways, for this hardy flower is one of the most prolific and easiest to grow. Marigolds generally thrive in poor soil and, after blooming, can reseed for the coming year. Claudia and Frieda order the marigold seeds to finance a bicycle, but after hearing their community's consensus that Pecola's baby would be better off dead, they elect to sacrifice the two dollars they have earned and plant the unsold seeds as a sign of their earnest prayers for the baby's survival. To Claudia, this child with "clean black eyes . . . flared nose, kissing thick lips, and the living breathing silk of black skin" is infinitely more desirable than a lifeless doll (148). Being drawn to Pecola's baby is also a means to "counteract the universal love of white baby dolls, Shirley Temples, and Maureen Peals," in other words, a means of affirming the baby's individual value (148). Planting their seed in "black dirt," indicating its apparent richness, Claudia and Frieda expect the marigolds to sprout in token that the baby will live (9). Nothing, however, germinates:

> Quiet as it's kept, there were no marigolds in the fall of 1941. We thought, at the time, that it was because Pecola was having her father's baby that the marigolds did not grow. A little examination and much less melancholy would have proved to us that our seeds were not the only ones that did not sprout; nobody's did (9).

Claudia's words imply that a dark season will ensue for everyone.

With Pecola representing African-Americans, the story is essentially about black identity, racial self-discovery. Morrison's nature imagery underscores the potential richness of the black soil. But the cultural climate in 1941 is sterile, with black men being drafted into the still segregated U. S. armed services and being given the most menial of duties. The picture of Pecola picking through garbage reflects the kinds of jobs which have historically fallen to black Americans. The Bluest Eye illustrates the possible consequences of entirely depending on external conditions for self-image, for in attempting to satisfy a paradigm that differs so radically from reality, African-Americans may destroy their essential nature. And in denying their natural gifts (or, as Morrison calls it, their "funkiness") in order to placate white expectations, African-Americans accelerate their self-destruction.

Morrison emphasizes her conclusion by opening *The Bluest Eye* with a paragraph from a child's reader: "Here is the family. Mother, Father, Dick, and Jane live in the green and white house. They are very happy" (7). This epigraph or, more precisely, thematic heading, is repeated twice, each time becoming more chaotic as punctuation, capitalization, and spacing disappear until the final version appears totally incomprehensible. Morrison's ironic contrast of this white, middle class ideal with its inverted image in the black community indicates an increasing degree of destruction, for the household which most aspires to imitate the one belonging to Dick and Jane, Geraldine's, is inimical to a healthy self-image. The claim by one critic that Geraldine's home is merely a "counterfeit of the idealized home" seems a bit misleading because the only surviving feeling in her home is anger.[15] And while Junior's sanity may not be as impaired as Pecola's, his self-expression through sadistic acts indicates a self-image only marginally better, particularly since he focuses his anger exclusively on the helpless. If Junior is the product of a home "that draws near this ideal" of whiteness, then the entire country is in trouble.[16]

Morrison uses her domestic paradigm mainly to focus attention on the difference between being brought up in white America as opposed to growing up in black America.[17] Using identical elements—house, mother, father, brother, sister, dog, and cat—Morrison shows the shameful reality existing for many African-Americans, with an abandoned storefront replacing the pretty house. The Breedlove family is ironic as their name, with Father a drunk, Mother an absentee, Brother a chronic runaway. The only cat in Pecola's life is the one Junior throws on her. The only dog is Old Bob, whom she poisons. Several additional uses of this story also shed light on the novel's themes. Various chapter headlines, fragments of the initial paragraph which serve as subject introductions to particular chapters, have a breathless quality, much like a child's chant to dispel ugly demons. And the incomplete endwords ("pretty," "happy," "play," and "laugh," ending as "P," "H," "pla," and "LA") generally deal with the qualities absent in Pecola's life. Morrison's final use of the story occurs in the internal dialogue between blue-eyed Pecola and her admiring friend, also Pecola. Here, Morrison completes the endword "play," which becomes a poignant echo of its previous appearance, the chapter climaxing after Junior's invitation to play.

Other than the ironic reflective play of the Dick and Jane story, the primary reflection belongs to Claudia, who looks at Pecola and sees her both as representative and scapegoat, who understands that Pecola is a needless victim in a world eager to manufacture reasons for her failure:

> This soil is bad for certain kinds of flowers. Certain seeds it will not nurture, certain fruit it will not bear, and when the land kills of its own volition, we acquiesce and say the victim had no right to live. We are wrong, of course, but it doesn't matter. It's too late (160).

Certainly for Pecola it is too late. But for Claudia, able to understand *why* instead of simply *how* Pecola became a victim, there is an even more intense urge to transcend the enervating image imposed on minorities, to derive strength and momentum from Pecola's sad example, and to develop a strong self-image, a whole.

Chapter 3

Sula

After completing *Sula* in 1973, Morrison says that she knew she was a writer.[1] And as an indicator of talent, depth, and stylistic innovation, *Sula* assures Morrison's literary reputation. Superficially, the novel seems a continuation of themes and structures introduced in *The Bluest Eye*. Again, Morrison uses paired female characters; themes of identity, love, and responsibility; a vivid sense of community; shifting narrative perspectives; and rich use of irony and paradox. But *Sula* challenges readers in ways *The Bluest Eye* does not, primarily because of Morrison's presentation of evil and the structures she employs to reveal its polymorphic nature.

Divided into two roughly equal parts, with a prologue followed by chapter titles consisting of dates, *Sula* appears to move in a straightforward progression from 1919 to 1927 and then from 1937 to 1941, with "1965" as the novel's epilogue. But the events of various chapters don't necessarily occur during the dates indicated; indeed, the text spirals and laps back on itself, accruing sometimes changing or contradicting meanings as it goes. This demands the reader's concentrated effort, for Morrison here dramatizes her talent for using language as "both indicator and mask."[2] *Sula* insists that readers put aside conventional expectations to enter a fictional world deliberately inverted to reveal a complex reality, a world in which evil may be a necessary good, where good may be exposed for its inherent evil, where murder and self-mutilation become acts of love, and where simple answers to ordinary human problems do not exist. *Sula* has drawn many critical essays that have attempted to give it a systematic, philosophically centered reading. But it defies single authoritative readings in theme and structure (although existential, Manichaen, and "other" readings come close) mainly because this is a novel about becoming and changing, sometimes in clear process, sometimes not.[3]

Sula's prologue begins by emphasizing place, indicating that the neighborhood of the Bottom, destroyed to make room for a golf course, will play a significant role in this narrative. The Bottom is more than a setting, however. Morrison often uses community as an active character in her work.[4] From the very start we are made immediately aware of a mythological dimension, drawn into an imaginative place where nature and people interact, as they often do in folk and fairy tales. Beginning with the end of the Bottom, Morrison introduces a pattern of inversion which she quickly succeeds with others. This includes the anecdote about the origin of the Bottom as a "nigger joke," when a white slave owner rewards his diligent slave with poor, hilly land where living will always be difficult.[5] This "joke," based on deceit and motivated by greed, becomes an important structural and thematic thread in *Sula*, for all of its elements bear directly on the lives of the Bottom's inhabitants. Behind the scenery, as it were, is the white man, controlling the literal disposition of the land and the slave's perception of it through the manipulation of language:

> "See those hills?   That's bottom land, rich and fertile."
> "But it's high up in the hills," said the slave.
> "High up from us," said the master, "but when God looks down, it's the bottom . . . of heaven—best land there is" (5).

The "joke" effectively isolates the slave and ensures his economic failure while reinforcing the owner's sense of superiority. At the same time, however, the slave gleans some measure of success from his choice, developing a sense of humor as grimly ironic as his daily existence. Thus while the white folks hear the later inhabitants' laughter, they remain ignorant of the pain "somewhere under the eyelids" (4).

Isolated by location, race, and economics, the Bottom develops into a neighborhood, sharing some values with nearby white Medallion and developing its own distinctive attitudes as well. Chief among them in the novel is the neighborhood's acceptance of evil, which seems a form of passive acceptance: "they let it run its course, fulfill itself, and never invented ways either to alter it, to annihilate it or to prevents its happening again. So also were they with people" (89-90). This sense of endurance, superficially so stoical, perhaps even rational in the face of oppression, may also be a form of fatalistic indifference or fear. In any case, it becomes self-defeating, because it may be concluded that their "view of survival and of Nature exists only on the physical plane and is rooted in the fear of dying rather than in a desire to live."[6] Fear leads Shadrack, most prominently, and other characters as well, to create external structures and focus on these instead of actual causes. Thus National Suicide Day, Shadrack's means of imposing order over fear, not death, becomes the structure which eventually assumes its own independent importance. This need for finding an objective correlative for fear will lead the community to focus its fear and hatred on the River Road, the tunnel, and on Sula for their perceived inherent evil while remaining blind to the mysterious and protean nature of evil.

Another character motivated by fear is Helene Wright. Hers is a fear of life, suggested by her attitude toward sexuality. Raised by her grandmother in a house guarded by four Virgin Marys, Helene is cautioned against "any sign of her mother's wild blood" (17). Helene escapes New Orleans' sultry atmosphere and her prostitute mother's shadow by marrying Wiley Wright and moving to Ohio, where she sets a standard for communal rectitude, a standard she later imposes on her daughter Nel. But Helene's existence seems more a denial of a former life than an affirmation of an improved one, especially when her veneer of dignity dissolves into a "brilliant smile" aimed at a loathsome white conductor who denigrates her at the beginning of a trip back to New Orleans. Helene's smile, a flirtatious appeal for understanding, allows Nel to see her mother in an entirely new context. No longer a woman "who could quell a roustabout with a look" but instead an image of "custard," Helene reveals an unsuspected side. The "custard" and "jelly" Nel associates with her mother suggest more than weakness (22). They reveal the nature of Helene's sexual fear.[7]

Nel's trip to New Orleans gives her a glimpse of another, more complex reality rife with paradox and denial. Her grandmother's parting injunction, "Voir," is a message to see and inspect (27). Helene refuses to translate for her daughter. Nonetheless, Nel returns to the Bottom aware of her separate identity: "I'm me. I'm not their daughter. I'm not Nel. I'm me. Me" (28). Contemplating her separateness, Nel wants two things out of life, to be "wonderful" and to leave Medallion (29). Now she is prepared to ignore her mother's objections and become best friends with Sula.

Sula's upbringing in her grandmother Eva's house is the most significant factor in developing her attitudes, her perceptions of life forming in the irregular house her grandmother designs. A microcosm of the Bottom, Eva's house contains all the elements of the larger community: love, lust, generosity, possessiveness, evasiveness, duty, tenderness, denial, and deceit. Both life-sustaining and moribund, Eva's house is a monument to her twisted sense of responsibility, a sense warped by dire circumstances.

Abandoned one November by her husband Boy Boy, Eva struggles to feed her three starving children until, sensing futility, she leaves them with a neighbor and disappears. Eighteen months later, Eva returns, with one leg missing but with notable prosperity, to reclaim her children and build her own home. Precisely how Eva loses her leg becomes the topic of speculation in the Bottom, though it is suggested that Eva sacrifices it in a train accident for an insurance settlement. Whatever the case, Eva's experience changes her from a passive victim to an active manipulator. Her motive shifts from love to hatred: "Hating Boy Boy she could get on with it, and have the safety, the thrill, the consistency of that hatred as long as she wanted or needed it to define and strengthen her and to protect her from routine vulnerabilities" (36). Finding an embodiment of evil, a locus for her hatred, Eva participates in the community's use of fear and hatred as a defining, strengthening, and protective emotion, and her reaction brings her positive results. Later, the residents of the Bottom will hate Sula, and their reactions against her will temporarily lead to caring relationships. Eva's hatred also frees her from conventional solutions to routine problems. She becomes "creator" and "sovereign" of her home, directing the lives about her with unquestioned authority (30). In effect, Eva assumes godlike proportions, her removed authority indicative of emotional distance, her power over life and death unchallenged.

We see the results of Eva's authority throughout the novel, especially in relation to male characters: the deweys, Tar Baby, and Plum. All receive Eva's care and all, to some extent, become her victims. Eva's rescue of the deweys from indifferent mothers is fraught with paradox. While they doubtless benefit from whatever care they receive, these boys, originally so different in age and physical features, live down to Eva's leveling assessment: "What you need to tell them apart for? They's all deweys" (38). As if Eva's initial dismissal of individuality arrests their development, the deweys never grow to physical or emotional maturity. Tar Baby, a white man boarding in Eva's house, receives similar treatment. Intent on drinking himself to death, he finds the shelter and indifference to his habits he requires in Eva's house.

This isn't so with Plum, Eva's only son, who grows up "floated in a constant swaddle of love and affection" (45). Here is another verbal paradox, with "floated" and "swaddle" suggesting Plum's perpetual infancy is brought to an abrupt end with military service in World War I. A year after his return to the United States, Plum appears in the Bottom with a "sweet, sweet, smile" induced by his heroin habit (45). Like Shadrack, Plum seems to have suffered a psychic war injury which he cannot relate. His silence and ever deeper withdrawal into drug induced euphoria finally spur Eva into action.

The scene during which Eva sets fire to Plum is suggestively political. Plum's drug habit along with military service and his discharge without adequate treatment echo Shadrack's premature release from a veteran's hospital. Both become casualties in a war which brings African-Americans no gain whatsoever. Thus the cherry pie and *Liberty* magazine assume ironic meaning and widen the significance of Plum's death. As the agent of death, Eva acts primarily out of love. Tears stream down her face as she tightly holds Plum. Grieving yet resolute, Eva's choice of death by fire echoes other mythic literary deaths and suggests purification and even rebirth, particularly with the references to "a wet light" and "some kind of baptism" (47). But Plum neither rises from his own ashes nor does he emerge from the flame strengthened and sanctified. He is extinguished by his own mother. No one questions Eva's act, certainly not the community which never believes the rumors it circulates. Only Hannah can summon the courage to ask her mother why she killed Plum. The response Hannah hears in "two voices" suggests at least two reasons. Eva's primary motivation is to allow Plum "to die like a man" instead of retreating further into drug-induced infancy (like Tar Baby), and here Eva's motive becomes self-protective, not liberating (72). Dreaming that Plum is trying to reenter her womb, Eva saves herself ("Godhavemercy, I couldn't birth him twice") and her idea of what Plum should be (71). Her act both destroys and saves.

Doubtless, Eva's notion of manhood relates to her practice of "manlove," a love of maleness for its own sake," which she passes on to her daughters (41). Here, too, we trip over another paradox. Though "prejudiced about men" to the extent that she flatters their egos and criticizes wives she deems short of domestic devotion, Eva never allows herself to become the mere object of masculine attention (42). What can be truthfully said is that she is like Hannah in that both "exist as sexually desiring subjects rather than objects of male desire."[8] But "manlove," the privileging of men, binds Eva to the community, cementing her to an unchallenged tradition—unchallenged, that is, until Sula reaches adulthood.

Structurally, Morrison prepares her readers for her title character through her use of inversion and paradox. Sula's delayed appearance also suggests the importance of all that precedes her in life: the Bottom, Shadrack, Helene, Eva. Thus when readers first encounter Sula savoring the "oppressive neatness" of Helene Wright's house, we know her background yet little about her (29). Morrison will continue this pattern throughout the novel, removing Sula from narrative action—with calculated results.

Just as Helene is surprised by Sula's acting contrary to expectations, readers should not anticipate conventional behavior from this elusive character. Morrison created Nel and Sula to be a whole: "Each has part of the other. . . . But each one lacked something that the other one had."[9] This lack, like Sula's absences, serves to define her and is first dramatized in the novel when Sula hears her mother saying, "I love Sula. I just don't like her" (57). Hannah's statement unwittingly severs a significant bond with Sula. Sula is conscious only of "a sting in her eye," but the event essentially points out Sula's difference from her mother (57). Sula and Nel immediately strengthen their union in a wordless ritual, loaded with sexual implications. But the hole they dig, both womb and grave, signals both their union and dissolution.

Chicken Little's death, which immediately follows, becomes central to the narrative because it serves to bind the girls closer together. This accident occurs at a critical age for these twelve year olds, pointing out their moral development. With Chicken's unexpected disappearance, Nel registers the first reaction: "Somebody saw" (61). This apparent fact prompts a fearful yet determined Sula to investigate. Her discovery of Shadrack's unexpected neatness momentarily distracts Sula until she observes him in his doorway. Sula cannot voice the frightening question ("had he?"), and Shadrack gives her an answer ("always") full of ambiguity (62). When Sula returns to Nel, the one on whom she depends for thought, Nel denies Sula's responsibility: "It ain't your fault" (63). Not only that, Nel seems equally distressed about Sula's missing belt, somehow equating one with the other. Nel's response suggests her own lack, a denial of her responsibility, despite the fact that she clearly represents communal responsibility throughout the novel. Her reaction seems self-contained, even detached. By contrast, Sula's soundless grief is eloquently directed at Chicken's misfortune, not her own. Absolved of responsibility, she nevertheless loses something central to her becoming whole. The test points out clearly what happened to her: "ever since her mother's remarks sent her flying up those stairs, ever since her one major feeling of responsibility had been exorcised on the bank of a river with a closed place in the middle. The first experience taught her there was no other that you could count on; the second that there was no self to count on either. She had no center, no speck around which to grow" (118-119). Sula fails to see this for many years, of course. It's far too early for such sophisticated introspection. But her later actions, especially her cool observation of Hannah being burned, underscore Sula's difference, a difference later termed "evil" by the community when it watches the result of this lack.

The contrasting characters of Nel and Sula seem to retain their balance for years to come. Indeed, Sula returns after a decade's absence knowing that she has missed Nel all along. It is Nel, not Sula, who has separated, despite the fact that Sula has been physically absent. Yielding to Jude Green's need for a "hem," a someone "sweet . . . to shore him up," Nel discovers a feeling stronger than her friendship (83). And in marrying a man who believes that the two can make one whole and complete Jude, Nel virtually extinguishes her possibilities for developing an independent self.

The images attached to marriage in *Sula* are far from complimentary, with this social institution literally signaling the

marriage - symbolizes
death of femininity
38 Toni Morrison's World of Fiction

death of the female imagination and individuality. "Those with husbands," the text says, "had folded themselves into starched coffins, their sides bursting with other people's skinned dreams and bony regrets. . . . Those with men had had the sweetness sucked from their breath by ovens and steams kettles" (122). Jude's concern all along is with himself, not Nel, as he longs for confirmation of manhood denied him through racist employment restrictions. In acceding to Jude's urging, Nel joins the community's valuation of females as significant support, not independent beings. Accepting her role as wife and mother, Nel never questions the quality of her life. Any urge to examine, any incentive to leave the Bottom, or even rebel against its traditions, leaves with Sula. It does not, however, return with her.

Following Sula's return, Nel briefly rediscovers another way of seeing: "It was like getting the use of an eye back, having a cataract removed" (95). But she is alone in celebrating Sula's reappearance. From the beginning, Sula irritates the Bottom with her individuality, her refusal to accept a woman's role. Without calling attention to the fact, Morrison gives Sula license to act as she pleases. Significantly enough, Sula can be said to behave "like a man. She's adventuresome, she trusts herself, she's not scared. And she is curious and will leave and try anything." Because of this "quality of masculinity," she is seen as a "total outrage."[10] Thus it's not surprising for a community held together in part by traditions largely maintained by and relating to women to label Sula "devil" and "pariah" (117, 122). To the Bottom, she is the embodiment of evil. And what actions illustrate the nature of her evil? She places Eva in a nursing home, and she selects sexual partners from among married men. The rest is rumor.

Sula's reason for Eva's removal to a nursing home is based on self-defense. Immediately after entering Eva's house, Eva brings up two issues wholly antagonistic to Sula. She shows no gratitude (to Eva) and she has no husband or children. Their ensuing argument illustrates deeply opposed ideologies, with Eva maintaining a traditional view of Sula needing a husband and babies to "settle" her and Sula vigorously asserting her right to make herself and not be made by others (92). To any conforming pleasure, Sula says she's not yielding. "I'll split this town in two," she declares to Eva, "and everything in it before I'll let you put it [the fire of individuality] out!" (93). The fire image occurs naturally enough to Sula. Knowing that Eva has burned Plum,

Sula fears her. She later tells Nel about this fear, but Nel, like the rest of the community, refuses to believe the rumors of Eva's murder of her son. From Sula's perspective, putting Eva in a nursing home prevents another murder—Eva's or Sula's.

As for Sula's method of satisfying her sexual needs, Hannah's similar acts should be recalled. Of course, Hannah's sexual acts did not antagonize the women of the Bottom. The difference stems largely from Sula's refusal to flatter male egos and thus seemingly devalue the men and, by extension, their wives. Sula's motives, however, are different from Hannah's, who simply refused to do without some "touching every day" (44). The sexual act becomes for Sula an act of self-exploration and affirmation. Even Sula's early romantic fantasies forecast her sensual self-exploration, as she spends hours "galloping through her own mind on a gray-and-white horse tasting sugar and smelling roses in full view of a someone who shared both the taste and the speed" (52). Later, sex becomes a free fall into "a stinging awareness of the ending of things: an eye of sorrow in the midst of that hurricane rage of joy. There, in the center of that silence, was not eternity but the death of time and a loneliness so profound the word itself had no meaning" (123). In this state, Sula experiences her deepest feelings, deep enough to bring "tears for the deaths of the littlest things" (123). Her sexual partner is relatively unimportant. He merely serves as the means to her end, "the postcoital privateness in which she met herself, welcomed herself, and joined herself in matchless harmony" (123). Sula is consequently more intimate with herself than is ordinarily true of others, more knowledgeable about herself, more attuned to her own needs and desires. In the end, this inner intimacy, far from being evil, assumes a purity, signified by her association with rain.

Nel, on the other hand, has envisioned sex in terms of tangles and webs, snares for a struggling self as well as for others. Her concept of love and female sexuality is rooted in possessiveness. Thus when Sula, innocent of possessive love, takes Jude as a lover, Nel feels personally betrayed. So attached is her sexuality to her husband, Nel mistakenly believes that it departs with him. Though she grieves sexual emptiness, she fears looking at other men. Nel cannot see herself as Sula so clearly envisions her, a spider dangling by her own spittle, "more terrified of the fall than the snake's breath below" (120). Unlike Sula, Nel fears change. She tries to hide from the fact that change is a necessary

part of life. Without Sula's influence in her life, Nel's imagina-
tiveness, her sensual enjoyment is replaced by a "little ball of fur
and string and hair" (109). By excluding Sula from her life, Nel
successfully isolates her friend, but the result appears like an
ironic form of suicide.

Meanwhile, Sula finally meets a man who admires female independence. Bored by clinging women, Ajax is initially
drawn to Sula because he thinks that besides his mother "this
was perhaps the only other woman he knew whose life was her
own" (127). Equally weary of men unable to respect her intelligence, Sula finds attractive Ajax's "refusal to baby or protect her,
his assumption that she was both tough and wise" (128). Surprisingly to Sula, Ajax prefers her in the superior sexual position
during love making. In this position, Sula imaginatively mines
the layers of Ajax's being to discover his essence, thinking in
terms of precious metals, semi-precious stones, and life-giving
loam. But their love affair ends when Sula resorts to the conventional domestic signals: a clean bathroom and table set for
two. Worse, though, is Sula's invitation for Ajax to "lean on"
her (133). Instead, he pulls her under him one last time before
going to Dayton, leaving Sula stunned and empty.

Sula's thwarted affair with Ajax emphasizes the varying
concepts of female love in the Bottom. She might have become,
like Nel, subservient to a husband who sees his wife as someone
to absorb his pain and bear his children. Or she might subscribe
to Hannah's practice, which allows sexual pleasure but denies
emotional ties. Before reaching adulthood Sula has rejected the
former choice; otherwise she would never have left the Bottom.
And after loving Ajax, she finds Hannah's approach equally unsatisfactory. Both concepts preclude mutual responsibility, the
former by making women entirely responsible for domestic
harmony, the latter by negating emotional connections. Sula's
aborted love affair also dramatizes how her capacity for affection
is consistently stifled. Looking back, she could trace a pattern of
emotional connection followed by loss. Chicken dies, Nel denies
her, and Ajax leaves. Looking at Ajax's drivers' license and seeing the name Albert Jacks, Sula discovers that she never knew
the identity of her lover. "And if I didn't know his name, " she
thinks to herself, "then there is nothing I did know and I have
known nothing ever at all since the one thing I wanted was to
know his name . . ." (136). In Eva's former bedroom, facing her
own as well as the evidence of her grandmother's futile expres-

sion of love, Sula might reflect on the insolvency of human relations. Unlike Nel, she doesn't expect either reward or punishment for her acts. She believes that "Being good to somebody is just like being mean to somebody. Risky. You don't get nothing for it" (144-45). Still, confronting death, Sula seems satisfied that she at least lived her own life, that perhaps her way has been good.

Sula dies as she lived—alone. Alive, her impact on the Bottom had been ironically positive since in reacting to Sula's presence adults became more cherishing of their elderly parents, mothers more vigilant over their children, and wives more caring with their husbands. Their actions, however, seem generated more from spite than love. Consequently, after Sula's death, the Bottom's residents revert to their former habits of neglect. No one claims that evil dies with Sula. The community's projection of evil on one resident and subsequently on a public works project proves ludicrous from the beginning. Signalling the fact that Sula's nature is not actually evil are her eyes, "clean as rain" (52). What, then, is her "problem?" An omniscient observation concerning the essence of Sula's nature suggests that she was dangerous, like Cholly Breedlove, because of an "idle imagination": "Had she paints, or clay, or knew the discipline of the dance, or strings; had she anything to engage her tremendous curiosity and her gift for metaphor she might have exchanged the restlessness and preoccupation with whim for an activity that provided her with all she yearned for" (121).

Sula's energy and intelligence go unrecognized and unemployed, ignored by a community too busy foisting its guilt and failure on her. This is distressing, as is the fact that Sula cannot overcome overwhelming odds to discover the necessary form of self-expression. Here, then, is an example of true evil in the story, coming from the waste of Sula both by herself and those around her. Without Sula upon whom to focus blame, the people of the Bottom shift to a tunnel, part of a local federally funded road project which has raised and then frustrated residents' hope for employment. Here we see further examples of evil in the forms of sexism and racism. What may be concluded is that if the story indeed "considers the ways in which society denies women the possibility of autonomy and independence," then the tunnel suggests the larger frame of how white Medallion (and by extension the United States) denies the same to an entire race.[11] Joining Shadrack on National Suicide Day, residents march to the tunnel and assault it with bricks and lumber. Of those who enter, many die as the tunnel collapses with Shadrack standing above " . . . ringing, ringing his bell" (162). That the tunnel, which becomes a grave to so many, has been built by whites seems no accident.[12]

The image of Shadrack presiding over the Bottom's death brings to mind John Donne's famous statement: "Any man's death diminishes me, because I am involved in Mankind; And therefore never send to know for whom the bell tolls; It tolls for thee." The obvious point of this image is to affirm the inter-relationship of all. Throughout *Sula* we are reminded of the impersonal interest with which the white community observes occurrences in the Bottom, interest similar to that of Nel and Sula as they watch Chicken and Hannah die. As observers, all remain fascinated yet detached from the fatal activity before their eyes. These reactions emphasize their inability to empathize with and their denial of responsibility for others. Significantly, it is Nel, representing the community, who has never consciously admitted her interest and role in Chicken's death. A visit to Eva in 1965 offers her a glimmer of truth as she is forced to review her role. What bothers her is that Eva "didn't say *see*, she said *watched*." An inner debate follows: "'I did not watch it. I just saw it.' But it was there anyway, as it always had been, the old feeling and the old question. The good feeling she had had when Chicken's hands slipped. She hadn't wondered about that in years. 'Why didn't I feel bad when it happened? How come it felt so good to see him fall?'" (170). The more Nel ponders these questions, the closer she comes to recognizing that Sula and she are intimately bound, despite her feeling of separateness, her relief over surviving.

Morrison presents a parallel catharsis to emphasize the importance of communal responsibility. Blaming Sula and the tunnel will not improve conditions any more than personal evil can be exorcised by death because the human community's problems remains more fundamental. As she does in *The Bluest Eye*, Morrison alludes to the human soil, the conditions for growth and development critical for nurturing healthy human beings through love unblighted by possessiveness or self-sacrifice, love allowing feelings for oneself as well as for others. Seeing the painful, disfiguring effects of love, Sula creates herself in her own image, becoming totally "free." But she does not become "free" in a positive way. About personal freedom Morrison herself has said that "ideally" it means "being able to choose your responsibilities. Not not having any responsibility, but being able to choose which things you want to be responsible for."[14] In shunning responsibility for the creation of a healthy community, white Medallion and the Bottom become culpable, not Sula. After all, she has little choice of her growing environment. Indeed, the extended neglect of children throughout the novel is a recurring reminder of communal dereliction. Chicken, the deweys, Ajax, Teapot, and Sula herself are allowed to grow with little supervision or care. No wonder that the children who survive become as self-centered as their adult examples. Sula's solipsistic approach may seem to be more extreme than that of others. But when we see the widening rings of denial moving out from her to the Bottom to Medallion and the rest of the United States, we begin to fathom the political depth of this novel. Sula at least wholly claims her life, including its failures, while others deny their human connections in favor of simpler, safer ways.

The community of the Bottom never recognizes its moral insolvency, never sees the role it plays in its destruction. But Nel is given a belated chance for self-recognition. Her glimpse of truth is brought about first when Eva, to whom Nel has paid a duty call, confuses Nel with Sula and soon thereafter asks how Nel managed to kill Chicken. Nel's assured moral rectitude melts as she begins to see that everyone might have been wrong about Sula, that what Sula stood for was not necessarily bad. In an exchange just prior to her death, Sula has pointed out her position to Nel:

> "How you know?" Sula asked.
> "Know what?"
> "About who was good. How you know it was you?"
> "What you mean?"
> "I mean maybe it wasn't you. Maybe it was me" (146).

Years later, Nel sees that Sula might have been right. Moreover, Nel acknowledges that there was spite behind communal actions, not love or moral conviction. And when she understands this, Nel also recognizes that Eva was right to confuse her with Sula. She sees that despite their difference, they were identical in their disclaimer of responsibility.

The story ends with the beginning of Nel's painful comprehension that much of what she has believed in has led her away from herself instead of leading her to truth.[15] Morrison's dramatization of tradition's unperceived barriers to self-discovery reflects her belief in the need for experimenting with life, of breaking rules, not simply out of boredom or curiosity but because there is no other way to explore possibilities. Sula discovers the terror and thrill of the free fall into life through her own creative capacity for invention. Nel, on the other hand, values duty and tradition more than self. Taught to believe in the virtue of self-sacrifice, she denies her own possibilities and becomes dependent on others for her life's meaning, and even, as Sula points out, for her own loneliness. Trying to read *Sula* as an either/or proposition, that either Nel or Sula must be right, is unnecessarily simplifying and distorting of this novel, for Morrison all along intends both characters to command our attention. Like the characters, labels of "good" and "evil" become confused because "one can never really define good and evil. It depends on what uses you put it to. Evil is as useful as good is."[16] And though what remains of the Bottom will never know that Sula was not what they thought her to be, at least Nel breaks through the barriers of traditional moral certainty to recognize a Sula she hasn't seen for a long time: "'We was girls together,' she said as though explaining something" (174). Her reference to girlhood recalls a time of their greatest possibility, a possibility Nel rejected in favor of conventional ideas about womanhood which in turn blinded her to the truth of Sula.

Nel's grief brings the novel to a close, but like most elements of the novel, it paradoxically opens up her own possibilities. Thus in a way, the novel is open-ended. Finishing *Sula*, we have to consider carefully what we in fact do know. Our conventional expectations, after all, have been challenged through omission, contradiction, paradox, irony, and speculation, through a fusion of supernatural and realistic, and through a lean prose conjuring gothic events. By the end, we are prone to have given up any dualistic thinking in favor of the fluid, multiple process Morrison's novel gives us. The novel and the title character require imaginative exploration into the nature of life and art. Ultimately this means that, artistic structure notwithstanding, we are asked to respond to the free fall into individual consideration instead of relying upon literary conventions.

Chapter 4

Song of Solomon

When Milkman Dead hurls his body at his best friend and mortal enemy Guitar Bains at the end of *Song of Solomon*, he enters the free fall into experience Sula lives. Unlike her, however, Milkman no longer feels detached from himself and his community. Indeed, his risk is a qualitatively different kind of experience, a paradoxically grounded leap of faith, for Milkman gains what Sula never consciously misses: a rich personal sense of cultural history connecting him to places, people, values, and a past that give life meaning and depth. Easily Morrison's most accessible novel, *Song of Solomon* draws upon several classical western literary traditions, specifically the theme of education, journey structure, and flight imagery. But Morrison's third novel, though incidentally similar to such important books of black literature as *Invisible Man, Manchild in the Promised Land,* and *The Cheneysville Incident,* differs because of her individual mix of conventions with originality. In *Song of Solomon,* Morrison stirs together folk and fairy tales, magic and root medicine, history and imagination for a distinctive fictional concoction.

Song of Solomon may at first read like many other examples of the *bildungsroman* genre, centering as it does on the education of Macon Dead III, called Milkman, as he searches for his meaning (identity) through discovery of his familial heritage and recognition of his human responsibility. Divided into two parts, *Song of Solomon* first focuses on Milkman's urban life in Michigan between 1931 and 1963 before sending him to the rural South in the second part to search for a reputed fortune he believes will free him from his family. Like many classical heroes,

Milkman undergoes a "miraculous" birth, miraculous in his case because he is conceived through magic and because he becomes the first black child born in Mercy Hospital. By contemporary American standards, Milkman is nobly born, descended from American aristocrats, property owners. Moreover, Milkman assumes the classic hero's journey of separation, initiation, and return.[1] Thus the novel's main theme and structure seem familiar even as Morrison reshapes them, giving them new dimensions.

The novel's first scene, so vivid in color and movement, sets in place virtually all the important elements we as readers will encounter: the flight motif, naming as a means to power, song, history, magic, and all the genuinely important characters in Milkman's life. Conspicuously absent is Milkman's father, Macon Dead II, who will remain in the novel's background, emotionally distant, greedy, and spiritually dead. Macon is not the father alluded to in Morrison's epigraph ("The fathers may soar / And the children may know their names") but he does provide an important link to the one in question.

Morrison's epigraph introduces us to the two most significant motifs in *Song of Solomon*, flight and naming. Reading this novel, we are struck by the preponderance of biblical names, beginning with the novel's title. Primarily a love poem, the biblical "Song of Solomon" celebrates union, specifically through the marriage of Solomon to a Shulammite maiden who is "black but comely."[2] Culturally, "Song of Solomon" is said to have "originated in the . . . ritual context of Passover," which celebrates the Israelites' liberation from Egyptian slavery, and this book has also been used to affirm God's love of African-Americans.[3] Morrison consciously draws upon all these cultural and historical allusions and adds still more. Like the biblical book, hers is a love song, a song also summarizing family history, which makes it akin to the griot's song. That the novel's song has deep African roots seems apparent in Morrison's choice of name, Solomon/Suliman, and the title may also pay tribute to her admired grandfather, John Solomon Willis. Another strong African link is implicit in Pilate's name, chosen by her illiterate father Macon Dead I (Jake) for its shape resembling "a tree hanging in some princely but protective way over a row of smaller trees."[4] In African mythology, trees often provide links between the living and spirit worlds, a role Pilate will fulfill.[5] Pilate's biblical name, freighted with irony, becomes appropriate as a pun. She will pilot Milkman to his true heritage. Other biblical names seem more in keeping with their characters, though never in a completely literal form. Ruth Foster Dead, like her biblical counterpart, is a loyal follower. But in following her father's and husband's wishes, she often enacts a form of resistance. Magdelene, First Corinthians, Rebecca (Reba)—these largely remain undeveloped characters, though Morrison will give flesh to Corinthians late in the novel. Most appropriate is the name Hagar. In the Bible Hagar was Sarah's handmaiden sent to Abraham before being cast away. Like her biblical namesake, Hagar becomes an outcast, banished by a bored lover, before losing herself in her own emotional wilderness.

Other names in this novel are accurately suggestive (Sweet and Circe) while some remain inaccurate or misplaced (Macon Dead, Sing), emphasizing the importance of learning the true name. Readers of classical literature might recall how often a true name provides the key to personal power and freedom, just as it will for Milkman. For African-Americans, the issue of names/identity/heritage may be infinitely complicated by the loss of an original family name, use of a former owner's name (an owner who might also be family), illiteracy, and/or clerical errors, as is the case of Macon Dead. Initially indifferent to names, Milkman will come to understand their importance: "When you know your name, you should hang on to it, for unless it is noted down and remembered, it will die when you die" (329). Unlike Guitar, who says that he doesn't care about names, Milkman sees that names "bear witness" (330). They have importance in themselves.

Milkman's own name, suggesting the interdependence of genders, is also a kind of demeaning joke, one he fails to understand for a long time. Dubbed "a natural milkman" by Freddie, his father's employee who witnesses Ruth nursing her four year old son, Milkman at first doesn't think about his name (15). Later, understanding its sexual implication, he embellishes it with meaningless conquests. Only late in the novel does he link his mother's nurturing with himself in a positive way, and then because he has learned to look at names as signs registering something more important underneath: "Under the recorded names were other names, just as 'Macon Dead,' recorded . . . in some dusty file, hid from view the real names of people, places, and things. Names that had meaning" (329). To look beneath the surface, Milkman must develop genuine interest—curiosity about what might be—involving a willingness to risk himself.

For much of the novel, Milkman exhibits neither interest, imagination, nor boldness. Indeed, we are told that when at the age of four Milkman learns "that only birds and airplanes could fly—he lost all interest in himself" (9). Though his birth is marked by flight, Milkman's life remains earthbound, weighted by competing ideologies held by the two most important men in his life, Macon and Guitar. Macon's faith in owning property as a measure of reality and self-importance is cut from the cloth of capitalism and materialism: "Own things," he says to his son, "then you'll . . . own yourself and other people too" (55). Guitar, on the other hand, sees race and gender as the primary determinants of reality: "Everybody wants the life of a black man," he declares (222). And his view of the world mirrors the limited nature of this perspective.[6] Thus Milkman's first flight seems conventional enough as he moves away from these earthbound ideologies. A young man, he wants to escape limits, including responsibility for himself and others. Lured by the possibility of instant wealth, he takes a plane from Michigan in search of Pilate's gold.

But rather than escape, as flight generally suggests, flight in *Song of Solomon* signifies a "spiritual passage."[7] It's a passage that charts his moves from adolescent solipsism and materialism toward a philosophy valuing even more the real treasures of family and heritage. From the very first the novel's emphasis suggests more spiritual than physical flight. As in the case of names, meaning lies beneath the surface. Not surprisingly, the connection between naming and flight reaches back into ancient literature, with flight often a reward for those who know the ancient or "true" name.[8] In this way, Morrison's use of the flight motif bridges Western with African mythologies, since both employ the flight metaphor.

Morrison also uses flight in *Song of Solomon* to suggest the outward rhythm of black men's lives.[9] She has pointedly stated how "attractive" she finds the ability of black men to leave their jobs and families, though equally aware that there can be a steep price to pay, particularly when that "price is the children."[10] Just as is the case in *Sula*, curiosity combines with courage leading to adventure. But while *Sula* ends with adventure, *Song of Solomon* goes further, showing how adventure becomes transmuted into story (song) and myth, linking past to present.

Milkman first awakens to family history through his

Aunt Pilate, whose name and reputation beckon the twelve year old boy and whose stories enchant him. Throughout the novel we are told many stories by different voices, relating character to character and past to present, unifying the many into one. Pilate, the "culture bearer," tells the best stories, though she has a close rival in Circe, a twin spirit.[11] Indeed, after hearing his aunt relate how his father saved her life and after meeting Hagar, Milkman "floats," lifted out of himself by a transporting personality (45). Pilate's stories form the nucleus of Milkman's integrating past, connecting him in unsuspected ways to those he already claims to know and some he doesn't. These stories inspire interest in others and provide a way for Milkman to discover where he might belong. He has no story of his own to tell, no song to sing, until he discovers the key word near the novel's end.[12] Then, having learned to listen and having found the key word—and in the process, an entirely different way of relating to people and places—Milkman can begin to think in terms of stories he might tell on his own.

Central to storytelling in *Song of Solomon* is Morrison's use of nature as a device to give the characters' stories the moral impact of fables.[13] The interplay between natural and unnatural in this novel expands Milkman's views and becomes integral to his moral development as it widens his interpretation of words. Pilate, for example, is held before him and everyone else as an example of an unnatural woman because she lacks a navel and because she refuses to dress and act in a culturally sanctioned feminine manner. But the metaphors applied to her consistently associate her with nature, undercutting communal value judgments. Both Pilate and Ruth are thought to have unnatural relationships with their fathers, relationships extending beyond their fathers' natural lives. However, both women find communication with their fathers' spirits both natural and life-sustaining.

Related to the issue of death and the dead as "unnatural" are race and murder, particularly racist attitudes leading to murder. The text of *Song of Solomon* is strewn with corpses, some fictional, others factual—all victims of racial violence. Whether or not this violence is natural depends upon perspective and language. Though Guitar finds murders committed by black people reasonable, and thus natural, he finds all white people "unnatural." Basing his judgment both on personal and national history, Guitar can point to numerous grotesque murders committed by white people "for fun" (156). Moreover, he asserts to Milkman, white people "know they are unnatural. Their writers and artists have been saying it for years. Telling them they are unnatural, telling them they are depraved. They call it tragedy. In the movies they call it adventure. It's just depravity that they try to make glorious, natural. But it ain't" (15). Guitar's very language demonstrates the slipperiness of the terms, equating "unnatural" with "depravity" and "natural" with "glorious." Characterizing the unknown or misunderstood as "unnatural" and using this judgment as an excuse for severing human relations plays as a theme with several variations throughout *Song of Solomon*.

But nature representing the natural world also serves a central role as Morrison reverses the traditional direction of her protagonist, sending him south, away from industrial "progress" toward rural primitiveness, to free himself. Part One of the novel, with its urban setting, is so far removed from the natural world that we are reminded of its presence only through Pilate. We become aware of the distance between natural and unnatural (industrial, civilized) worlds through Macon, who has once had a sustaining relationship with the earth but has channeled his father's urge to possess and cultivate his farm to an extreme. Macon sees his lifeless keys to rental property as "anchors" preventing his becoming "a landless wanderer" (27). Losing sight of his father's goal, Macon views wealth as an end in itself, more valuable than personal relationships. He marries Ruth for her father's wealth and social position, severs his ties with Pilate over gold, and urges Milkman to imitate his example by stealing from Pilate when his wealth has purchased nothing more than a spiritual death. Macon, as a recurring joke reminds us, is already Dead. His mortuary quiet house and "hearse" automobile silently comment on his state of being. Macon's one moment of spiritual ease occurs when he stands outside Pilate's house listening to her singing and recalls "fields and wild turkey and calico" (29). The further he travels from Lincoln's Heaven and his association with farming, forests, and the values implicit in both, the more unnatural he becomes. Pilate, on the other hand, embodies all that is truly natural. Her woodsy smell and pebbly voice, her easy association with earth and sky instruct Milkman in new ways of seeing. Still, he must undertake his own discovery of nature's value.

En route to Danville, Pennsylvania, Milkman sees the

countryside as "merely green" and "uneventful" (226-27). Once in Danville, however, Milkman learns that place is significant because it "makes the past real" (231). Nevertheless, his relationship to nature remains problematic not only because Milkman assumes superiority over it but also because he fails to pay attention to nature's language, just as he fails to heed Circe's advice implicit in her story of Butler greed and its path to ruin. Milkman leaves Danville with fewer tokens of earthly wealth, though still determined to find Pilate's gold. Once in Shalimar, Virginia, his education of nature intensifies. Almost immediately he sets himself at odds with its inhabitants by insulting them and then fighting. His pride injured and his manhood at stake, Milkman accepts an invitation to a hunt. He brags about his prowess despite the fact that he has no experience. But stripped of his three piece suit and dressed in worn hunting clothes, Milkman enters the woods outside Shalimar and almost immediately stumbles upon his uncharted self. For the first time he considers his behavior in relation to others and just exactly what he "deserves": "Under the moon, on the ground alone . . . the cocoon that was 'personality'—gave way. . . . There was nothing here to help him—not his money, his car, his father's reputation, his suit, or his shoes. . . . His watch and his two hundred dollars would be of no help out here, where all a man had was what he was born with, or had learned to use. And endurance" (276-77). Reduced to essentials for the first time in his life, Milkman begins to question his surroundings, and as he listens, noise becomes language, or rather "what there was before language" (278). His willingness to listen comes just in time to save his life from Guitar. Because he has reached back toward a time when humans and animals shared communication, Milkman comprehends a mythic dimension.

But while Milkman begins to perceive time as circular and mythic, Guitar remains convinced of its linear and historic structure.[14] The friendship of these men seems at first similar to that of Sula and Nel, but actually has the significant difference in that each remains complete in himself.[15] Rather than serving as the "moral center of the novel," their friendship illustrates diversity of character and personal choice.[16] Older than Milkman by five years, Guitar leads a very different life. A victim of racist devaluation of black life when his dead father's employer offers forty dollars and a bag of divinity as reparation, Guitar is uprooted from his southern home. Displaced again by Macon

Dead, who evicts Guitar's grandmother and the children she raises, Guitar remembers the lessons of poverty. Streetwise, adventurous, curious, and bold, Guitar is related to Morrison's other golden-eyed characters, Cholly Breedlove and Sula Peace, and like them he becomes "dangerously free," not because he denies social responsibility but rather because of his rigid definition of it.[17]

For much of the novel, Guitar's comments prick Milkman's idle conscience, pointing out his basic indifference to others. To Guitar, Milkman, with his fancy suits, expensive shoes, wealthy friends, and lack of feeling, is "not a serious person" (104). Because he has experienced the hard lessons of American racial politics, Guitar's vision of history and humanity narrows to the point where gender and race determine everything. His decision to join the Seven Days, a secret organization sworn to avenge the unprosecuted murders of African-Americans, suggests more, however, than radicalization. In the context of this novel, it suggests a moral subversion. As a child in Florida, Guitar existed as a natural hunter, living close to the earth and finding his joy in the chase, not the kill. Guitar's one hunting story ends with his deep remorse over shooting a doe. This conspicuous grief illustrates the depth of feeling he can have for other living things, both animal and human. It isn't surprising, then, that for much of the novel Guitar serves as Milkman's essential link to the Southside community, providing introductions and access, guiding his sheltered friend through living lessons, however lost they are on a bored and indifferent Milkman. Significantly enough, though, Guitar sees not only the human but also the political realities before him. Thus he justifies his decision to kill. He claims that he acts out of love, unable to see the potential for human indifference, though Milkman does. To be able to murder "indifferent as rain," Guitar eliminates most of his humane instincts and resorts to the age old "earthly solution to evil," murder.[18] Pressed by his own limited and limiting perspective, Guitar's vision becomes as deadly as Macon's. By imitating their oppressors, they become them. Thus Milkman's decision to reject the death-ridden influence of Guitar becomes an affirmation of life not only because of his perception of the corruption and fundamental injustice of Guitar's acts. However impersonal Guitar may claim murder to be, it has immediate consequences on both murderer and victim.

We see these consequences during Milkman's hunt with the men of Shalimar. This key scene pulls together many thematic threads, but it is especially important because Milkman finally begins to take responsibility for himself and his actions and in so doing comes to value life. His near death experience purges his self pity, for, ironically having become a real victim, Milkman no longer feels like one. His sense of victimization turns out to be a significant emotional link with Guitar, a link which, when broken, frees Milkman to walk upright instead of remaining crippled by limiting ideas of race and gender. Milkman completes his exorcism of Guitar during the ritual skinning and evisceration of the male bobcat shot during the hunt.[19] Through their communal dressing of the carcass, the hunters demonstrate respect for their kill. Observing each stage, Milkman hears a counterpoint of Guitar's self-serving rationalizations. His concluding justification is that all this has been "about love. What else?" (282). With "What else" echoing in his mind, Milkman literally sees the answer—death—before him. And as he removes the cat's heart, the peacock image recurs. Suggesting vanity and materialism, this time it flies away.

Free of his disabling vanity and acquisitiveness, Milkman's education nevertheless remains incomplete because he has neglected to recognize the significant role women have played in his life. As readers, we have been generally aware of these significant roles all along. But a close look at the types of female characters and the specific roles they play in the novel, especially in contrast to Pilate, gives a new dimension to the theme of education.

Because of her central role in the novel and because she is such a striking fictional creation, Pilate has inspired a variety of commentary, ranging from claims of her being the true hero of *Song of Solomon* to her playing a conventional supporting role.[20] Given Pilate's attributes, it's difficult to relegate her to the role of handmaiden to a questing hero. A self-delivered and self-sustaining figure of archetypal proportions, Pilate has no concern with finding herself; she *is* herself. From the age of twelve she carries her identity with her in an earring she devises from her mother's brass snuffbox. Her unique self-knowledge does not simply derive from awareness of her name, though Morrison consistently associates name choice, identity, and function throughout this novel. Instead, Pilate's self-awareness and self-confidence are the results of direct experimentation with life, not vicarious, imagined, or protected experience.

Even as a child Pilate enjoys an immediate and palpable contact with elemental life. Thinking of his sister, Macon remembers that she smelled like a forest and that she was "born wild" (166). He recognizes her as part of nature. Adored by her father and brother who admire her miraculous presence, Pilate grows unencumbered by anything remotely resembling a traditional feminine role. As a natural child, free to follow her own inclinations, Pilate relishes her freedom, roaming over her father's farm and the surrounding forests. Her sentient relationship with nature has its practical value. Because of this relationship, she and Macon are able to elude their father's murderers and survive in the wild. Pilate's intimacy with nature underscores her spiritual development, metaphorically linking her to other dimensions of reality. This close association literally allows her to see her father's ghost, which appears throughout her life to comfort and direct her.

Morrison emphasizes the connection between nature and contact with the spirits of the dead in several ways. First, she indicates that Macon, at the time of their father's murder as closely in tune with nature as Pilate, can also see his father's spirit. Secondly, Morrison relates their prescience through direct language: "The cardinals, the gray squirrels, the garden snakes, the butterflies, the groundhogs and rabbits—all the affectionate things that had peopled their lives ever since they were born became ominous signs of a presence that was searching for them, following them" (168). As Macon moves away from nature in his pursuit of wealth, he loses contact with his father. Pilate, however, continues a "close and supportive posthumous communication" with her father's spirit, an important compensation for her isolation from other human beings (139). Throughout her work, Morrison dramatizes interdependence among characters, going still further in *Song of Solomon* by indicating that wholeness derives in part from shared relationships between men and women. Pilate, in particular, benefits from "a dozen years of a nurturing, good relationship with men."[21] Such knowledge strengthens her throughout her life. Rather than "defining herself according to the standards and desires of a beloved male," Pilate gains self-assurance through love, a self-assurance which both Reba and Hagar lack.[22] Only Milkman will enjoy a similarly enabling love given by Pilate, a love given without expecting anything in return. It matters little that Pilate misinterprets her father's cryptic messages as requests to retrieve his bones. What matters is that his messages serve to connect her to the past and to the nurturing link with her father.

Pilate's lack of human connections, severed at first by death and human greed and later by unreasoning fear when people discover she has no navel, forces her to develop her own moral strength. She seems naturally endowed with a moral sense, strongly challenged when Macon kills a white man mistaken for their father's ghost and decides to take his gold. Pilate's opposition to Macon suggests not only the contrary directions their lives and values will take but also her personal determination. Doubtless she recognizes that enforcement of her will is bound to cost her the affection of the one person she loves in the world. Nevertheless, Pilate apparently feels her moral convictions more important than Macon's love. She never questions her choice. In fact, as succeeding episodes of human frailty test Pilate's moral sense, her convictions gain strength.

By the age of sixteen, she has witnessed her father's murder, broken with her brother, been sheltered then rejected by migrant workers, had a baby, and accepted responsibility for her part in a murder without support from anyone other than her father's ghost. No wonder, then, that Pilate grows angry with the people she encounters and with herself for the deceptions she invents to make herself acceptable. Recognizing that she cannot be other than she is, Pilate assesses herself, and then "when she realized what her situation in the world was and would probably always be she threw away every assumption she had learned and began at zero. First off, she cut her hair. That was one thing she didn't want to think about anymore. Then she tackled the problem of trying to decide how she wanted to live and what was important to her" (149).

In cutting her hair, Pilate sheds her most obvious sign of femininity and personal vanity, obstacles she wants to ignore. In fact, culturally defined femininity becomes irrelevant, as Pilate's androgynous clothing indicates. Her next decision, determining the manner of her life, is more complex and subject to change. Essentially, Pilate chooses to live a mobile, simple life. Restless by nature, Pilate wanders until, recognizing Hagar's need of a more conventional life, she stops to look for Macon. And though he refuses to accept her as part of his family, Pilate nevertheless settles close to Macon, first to create and then to protect and guide the remaining, fragile family link, Milkman. Addressing her needs, Pilate becomes a bootlegger because it allows her the greatest amount of freedom at the least personal expense, and she maintains the simplest of shelters, with neither running water nor electricity. Her unpretentious mode of living mirrors her values, reflecting her commitment to the essence of life instead of its artifices. Thus Pilate recognizes the importance of freedom, love, personal integrity, moral responsibility, human relationships, food, and song while ignoring material comforts.

The simplicity, beauty, and courage of Pilate's decisions reveal her to be the sanest, most honest, guilt-free and humane character in *Song of Solomon*. Ultimately Pilate represents a completely natural woman, undistorted by convention, expectations, disappointment, delusions, hatred, or resentment. Refusing to cast blame on either cultural or personal forces, Pilate accepts herself and others as she finds them. Rather than being molded by her culture, she forms herself, especially after discovering the insubstantial nature of others' fears. This brings us to Pilate's most prevalent feature, her absolute fearlessness. While other female characters of this novel fear some form of rejection, Pilate fears neither isolation nor its most permanent manifestation, death. Her active and sustaining relationship with her father convinces Pilate that death is not an insurmountable barrier.

Although these attributes qualify Pilate to guide, her example inspires few followers. Macon, for instance, remains blind to Pilate's value, placing his faith in property. With Milkman, however, Pilate's example bears fruit. Her simple life illustrates its potential richness, her insistence upon fairness evokes his sense of responsibility, her love demands his consideration. Consequently, at the end of *Song of Solomon*, Milkman will risk his life to save Pilate's and in so doing he will discover the courage which gives him wings.

Pilate guides not only through example but also by contrast. Throughout the novel, Morrison employs Pilate's individual strength as a foil for the conventional weaknesses of other female characters: Ruth, Lena, First Corinthians, and Hagar. With Hagar, Morrison especially contrasts the difference between the beneficial effects of Pilate's altruistic love with the destructive results of Hagar's possessive, blinding obsession. After her initial scorn turns into love, Hagar eventually loses all self-understanding. Allowing her passion to be taken for granted and surrendering her self-respect, Hagar smothers the little remaining interest Milkman has in her. Hers becomes a wasted life because she has no aim other than to be loved. This is partially a result of being spoiled by Pilate and Reba, who scurry to fulfill Hagar's desires. To her mother and grand-mother, Hagar remains a "baby girl" (319). But to Guitar, who sympathetically speculates on the cause of her obsession, Hagar is one of the "doormat" women, described in the text as "women who had been spoiled children. Whose whims had been taken seriously by adults and who grew up to be the stingiest, greediest people on earth and out of their stinginess grew their stingy little love that ate everything in sight" (306). Hagar's possessive love precludes all self-respect. In fact, her love denies any sense of self at all. Her only contact with herself comes from a mirrored reflection, leading her to a false and superficial assessment. Lacking perception and judgment, Hagar mistakenly assumes that Milkman leaves her for a more attractive nearly white girl. The "hollow eyes" of her image reflect more than emotional an-guish, however. They indicate Hagar's emptiness, for she is nei-ther encouraged nor forced to develop an independent sense of self or resiliency, the very strengths she so much admires in Pi-late. Hagar's "anaconda love" finally consumes her, leaving her without "self," "fears," "wants," or "intelligence" (137). Having erroneously assumed that Hagar needs only love to sustain her, Pilate fails to see her life "stumped" in two senses: its brevity and scope of development (319).

Ruth Foster Dead's life becomes similarly "stumped," though she describes herself as having been "pressed small" to fit first her father's conception of a dutiful daughter and later Macon's idea of an acceptable wife (124). She is encouraged, even at times coerced, into passive, quiet, and orderly behavior by her father, who continues to tuck Ruth into bed long after she becomes capable of going by herself. Then Ruth seems an ideal wife for Macon, who treats her like a doll, delighting in the act of undressing his wife (instead of in her). In direct contrast to Pi-late, a fully independent woman by the time she becomes six-teen, Ruth remains a child. Ruth's helplessness, domestic inep-titude, and blandness develop to protect her from the men in her life, who consider her only in terms of her usefulness to them. Throughout the novel, Ruth remains a nebulous figure, largely content to assert her individuality in apparently insignif-icant ways as opposed to Pilate's gigantic presence.

As an illustration of the effects cultural restraints have on women, the contrast between Ruth and Pilate becomes especially significant. Contained by the house her father builds to flaunt his success and position, a house her husband uses for the same reason, Ruth allows herself to be controlled to a large degree by their expectations of her. Their presumptions automatically relegate Ruth to a role of adoring, or at least docile, dependent. Her primary function is to bring comfort to male domestic life by maintaining the house, preparing meals, and not questioning authority. Though conspicuous, Ruth's domestic ineptitude gives rise only to complaints instead of investigation into and development of her true gifts. Significantly, though Macon chafes at the thought of his febrile wife, he raises his daughters to become like their mother.

The lives of Lena and First Corinthians, in their turn, are thwarted by Macon's expectations. As girls, they are "displayed then splayed" before others to arouse envy and to aggrandize Macon's self-image (216). Daily asserting his authority, Macon manages to keep "each member of his family awkward with fear" (10). And he pays little attention to the practical aspects of his daughters' futures, a painful lesson for Corinthians who later discovers that her Bryn Mawr education has "unfit her for eighty percent of the useful work in the world" (189). They are raised to become wives and then taught to see themselves as too fine for most eligible men. Thus when both Lena and Corinthians reach middle age, they are still making the red velvet roses indicative of their decorative function. These characters, however, gather strength during the course of the novel, as Morrison indicates by elaborating on Corinthians' growth in particular.

An integral part of the novel, Corinthians' development parallels Milkman's growth and encapsulates the struggle for identity described in Morrison's first two novels. Like Claudia MacTeer and Sula, Corinthians reaches a point in her life where she must choose between finding her own function or accepting the one prescribed for her. She must finally choose between following convention or challenging it, between living a sheltered life or risking it.

Two years before Pilate turns Milkman in the direction of his heritage and identity, Corinthians has taken inventory of herself. At forty-two, she realizes that she probably won't marry, that her liberal arts education is a practical hindrance, and that getting out of her father's house is more important than deteriorating in it. Partially overcoming her pride, she takes a job as the state poet laureate's maid, though she nevertheless maintains her illusion of superiority by misrepresenting the truth to her mother and by avoiding domestic dress. But Corinthians finds her job gives her responsibility where she "exchanged arrogance occasionally for self-confidence" (190). More important, her job brings her into contact with Henry Porter.

Corinthians' love affair with Porter becomes critical to her development because, for her to make an emotional commitment to him, she must discard the false assumption at the root of her life. She must discard her idea of superiority because of wealth and Porter's perceived social and intellectual inferiority because of his poverty. Having patiently waited for Corinthians to decide his importance in her life, Porter forces her decision with a firm ultimatum when she again uses Macon's disapproval as an excuse to avoid sexual intimacy. One night, driving her home, Porter says, "I don't want a doll baby. I want a woman. A grown-up woman that's not scared of her daddy" (196). At this point, Corinthians realizes that she doesn't know any grown-up women, including her self, and that her future without Porter will be a "smothering death of dry roses" (199). Thus, afraid that he will drive away from her life, she clings to Porter's car. The act allows her to pass through pride to humility, a path Milkman will later take in the Shalimar forest, the distance she travels marking a spiritual passage. Later, cleansed of debilitating fears, inhibitions, and snobbery, Corinthians feels "bathed," "scoured," and "simple" (199). Instead "of vanity she now felt a self-esteem that was quite new" (201). Like Pilate before her and Milkman after, Corinthians moves from her father's house to one she shares with Porter, indicative of her self-release from extended childhood.

Despite their apparently stunted or delayed emotional growth, Hagar, Lena, Corinthians, and Ruth serve important roles as guides, goads, and silent support in Milkman's education. Morrison, however, endows her female characters with more importance than conventional supportive roles. Their stories counter-balance male-centered stories, giving a widening perspective and taking into account a wholly differing point of reference. Milkman flees from Michigan, leaving behind women who have cared for and about him. Initially, escape seems all important as he thinks about the women he is leaving behind: "Lena's anger, Corinthians' loose and uncombed hair matching her slack lips. Ruth's stepped up surveillance. . . .

Hagar's hollow eyes—he did not know whether he deserved any of that, but he knew . . . he had to leave quickly" (220-21). Though he has dismissed Hagar from his life, she continues to haunt him through her spiritual forbearer Ryna. Hearing from Circe about Hagar's great-grandmother's "Nervous love," Milkman connects the two, and the more of Ryna's story he pieces together, the greater his understanding of Hagar until he reaches genuine remorse for his treatment of her (243). Although he returns too late to make amends, Milkman's acceptance of the shoebox containing Hagar's hair signifies his assumption of responsibility for her death.

Hagar serves as one spur for Milkman's departure; Lena the other. Incensed by Milkman's tattletale revelation of Corinthians' love affair to Macon, Lena confronts her brother with scathing truths about himself from a perspective he has ig- nored for thirty-two years: "You've been laughing at us all your life," she tells him. "Corinthians. Mama. Me. Using us, order- ing us, and judging us: how we cook your food; how we keep your house" (215). Ignoring his feeble protest, Lena continues, pointing out that his assumption of authority comes from "that hog's gut that hangs down between your legs" (215). His sex, she assures Milkman, is insufficient to ensure his superior position, not only because he has nothing else on which to base his domi- nance but also because she now claims her own rights. "I don't make roses anymore," she concludes, "and you have pissed your last in this house" (216). However shadowy Lena's presence in Milkman's life, she steps into light during this scene, demand- ing to be seen and heard.

Perhaps more than fleeing Hagar's obsessiveness and Lena's chafing unpleasantness, Milkman runs from becoming saddled with his parents' conflict. During the course of the novel, Milkman reluctantly hears two versions of why Macon hates Ruth. Macon's story assumes a decidedly incestuous slant, justifying both his early suspicions and later treatment of her. Ruth's version, stamped with her own need, attempts fairness. In any case, both stories fall on unsympathetic ears, because Milkman doesn't "want to know any of it" (76). Resentful of this emotional burden, he sees himself as his parents' undeserv- ing victim until, discovering the importance of human relation- ships, he reconsiders: "But why shouldn't his parents tell him their personal problems? If not him, then who?" (276). At this point, Milkman has still not bridged the last critical gap of sympathetic participation, of being able to see through others' eyes.

He doesn't arrive at this perspective easily, quickly, or alone. Significantly, a woman leads Milkman to discover another angle. After experiencing Sweet's liberating love, Milkman understands the joy of sharing. In her arms, he dreams of flight, a flight taking place not alone but in another's presence. It is Sweet to whom he first tells his family's story, and it is Sweet who asks the question forever tempering Milkman's marvel over his flying ancestor. "Who'd he leave behind?" she asks (328). Her question demands his acknowledgement of the price of flight and the view from the ground.

Sweet's question underscores Morrison's theme of shared history, development, and responsibility blind to limitations of gender and race, a theme she will continue to explore. No longer a bored, spiritually crippled, vain, and selfish adolescent, Milkman, having discovered the value of human relationships, reduces it to an essential question: "Would you save my life? or would you take it?" (331). Though he determines an answer in relation to his life, he doesn't consider his response to others until Guitar mistakenly shoots Pilate on Solomon's Leap. Again, she points the way, toward love and caring for others, taking flight even as she remains earthbound. Milkman's final gesture more than claims his life from Guitar. It affirms his relation to Solomon and Pilate, and joins them. A "lodestar" setting his own course, he meets them in their mythic and elemental flight.

Chapter 5

Tar Baby

In an interview following the publication of *Tar Baby,* her fourth novel, Morrison said that she had given herself "permission to write books that do not depend on anyone's liking them." She added that "a writer does not always write in the ways others wish." Apparently many people did actually wish that *Tar Baby* had been written differently, because it turned out to be Morrison's least popular work. In the same interview, Morrison indicated that instead of popularity what concerned her most was that "the writing gets better." Asked if she was satisfied that she was indeed continuing to grow as an artist, she took a look at her career and concluded that, yes, she could see some lines of development with the help of "hindsight." She noted that "from a book that focused on a pair of very young black girls, to move to a pair of adult women, and then to a black man, and finally to a black man and a black woman is evolutionary." Also, she thought that her writing was now marked with a finer sense of economy and structure and "more courage."[1] To these positive developments she might have added several more. For example, in *Tar Baby* she chose to employ a more dramatic as opposed to a heavily descriptive kind of writing. She dared to bring myth, legends, and folklore even more to the forefront, along with the African idea of a conscious nature. For the first time, she presented both black and white characters who play major roles. She extended her canvas, moving from the "village" setting typical of her first three novels to the Caribbean and beyond. Additional examples of her development could be cited. But let it simply be said that despite the great success of her previous novel, she was not tempted just to do more of the same. She was anxious to continue to grow, to perfect her writing as much as possible. Because of this deliberate aspiration, *Tar Baby* contains some of Morrison's very best writing, and comes off as something of a *tour de force*.

Perhaps the fact that *Tar Baby* does in fact often showcase Morrison's special abilities helps to explain better than anything else why it wasn't more popular with the reading public. Morrison challenged herself so consciously in this novel to do her best that she wound up with one of those novels that people tend to call "difficult." In other words, the meaning of the story wasn't plainly on the surface. The story had to be mined with an active imagination. A reader reflecting the impatience of this media-driven age would certainly miss the text's complex meaning. So would a reviewer rushing to meet a deadline. Thus, it was not surprising that, initially at least, the widespread impression advanced that Morrison had somehow lost control of her imaginative resources, and that *Tar Baby* was consequently a failure.

However, if *Tar Baby* was generally dismissed as a disappointment when it first appeared, that is no longer the case, at least not with most critics. During the intervening years, its reputation has steadily climbed. There remain those critics who continue to focus on the imperfections of the novel. Certainly, there are flaws. But they are essentially flaws of creative ambition. Sometimes Morrison stretches her writing almost to the breaking point, investing her novel with so many layers of aesthetic and thematic meaning that the text can show signs of strain. In this connection, there is no denying that at times *Tar Baby* has a "disjointed" quality that can be frustrating to the reader.[2] Nevertheless, in the final analysis, the flaws of *Tar Baby* are easily outweighed by the virtues of Morrison's ability to tell a complicated story dealing with some of the most paradoxical, clashing issues of our time.

Morrison's story opens with a fugitive, William "Son" Green, jumping ship and landing on a Caribbean island. The island belongs to Valerian Street, a wealthy candy manufacturer who has retired to his splendid home with his wife Margaret and his faithful black servants Ondine and Sidney. The Streets' only guest is Jadine Childs, Ondine and Sidney's niece who has been generously supported by Valerian since she was orphaned. Absent is the Streets' son Michael, though there is some hope he might show up for the approaching Christmas holiday. But instead of Michael, it is Son who shows up, looking for all the world like a dangerous criminal. After his discovery, things will never be the same for the occupants of Valerian's house. They all are shaken out of various states of complaisance that have allowed them to turn away from some uncomfortable truths. Jadine is most shaken because after initially feeling repelled by Son, she finds herself falling in love with him. Son is equally attracted to her. And so, after a Christmas dinner which ends in a kind of truth-throwing brawl between masters and servants, they decide to flee to New York, where they plan to start their life together. Their relationship, however, soon becomes strained, and a split inevitably occurs. The fatal truth is that they can't successfully live with or without each other. Son and Jadine are opposites in the most essential ways, incompatible in their personal hopes and dreams. On the other hand, they can't entirely let go of each other, as if stuck to a tar baby.

The "tar baby" folk tale endures as one of the most familiar stories to come out of the Uncle Remus series written by Joel Chandler Harris. In the tale, a farmer tries to trap a troublesome rabbit by placing a tar baby in the middle of the cabbage patch. The tar baby, dressed in a skirt and bonnet, looks attractive but is very sticky to touch. When the rabbit inevitably gets stuck to it, the farmer makes plans to destroy the troublesome pest. But the rabbit, ever resourceful, outwits the farmer at the last minute. "Boil me in oil," he pleads, "skin me alive, but please don't throw me in that briar patch." Wishing to do the worst thing to the rabbit, the farmer falls for the trick and flings the begging rabbit into the briar patch. The rabbit jumps up and calls out sarcastically "This is where I was born and bred at," and runs off "lickety-split." Morrison heard this tale, or variations of it, as a child, and it stayed in her imaginative memory until she decided to use it as the departure point and an organizing principle for her fourth novel.[3]

Some critics have complained that the Uncle Remus story doesn't work as a completely consistent analogue in Morrison's story, that the metaphoric framework of the folk tale isn't strictly applied.[4] But such complaints have no real critical foundation because Morrison never intended to employ Harris' tale in a strict way. Instead, she wanted to depend on her memory to recollect "the *told* story" of her childhood. In that way, she felt she would be closer to the original tale, whose source happened to be African. Also, by refusing to be deliberately guided by Harris' tale, or even to read a "Westernized version of the story," she felt she would be freer to employ material she was convinced could be especially useful, "the pieces that were disturbing or simply memorable."[5] In short, she never planned to make *Tar Baby* into a modern retelling of Harris' tale, even if at a crucial point the tale is directly invoked and some definite correspondences can be discovered throughout the novel.

In Morrison's story, Valerian Street can be seen to correspond in certain ways to the white farmer of the folktale. He owns the property disturbed by an outcast who scurries and sneaks around and steals food. Valerian's fortune has been built on a candy that is as sticky as tar, and he is the patron of a young woman who captures the invading thief with her attractiveness. But Morrison isn't interested in going much further beyond such correspondences. They function primarily as departing points for the issues that concern her. She prefers instead to depend on her characters to carry her ideas. Thus, the full meaning of the text is apprehended through the gradual revelation of the personalities and histories of her characters. Her characters, in turn, can't be fully appreciated unless it is remembered that they embody the main themes, and are therefore complicated, paradoxical human beings who clash with each other and with their other selves.

Valerian is perhaps the most paradoxical, split between being admirable and awful. On the admirable side, he has been a generous employer and something of a philanthropist. As the inheritor of the candy business, he was thrust into a position of power; but he retired as soon as he could, yearning for a more meaningful life than just having business success. On his retirement island, he has built a separate wash house to remind him of a childhood experience when, on the day he was orphaned, a black washer woman with heart emotionally touched him. He has also built a greenhouse where he spends his time raising flowers, listening to classical music, reliving memories, hosting spiritual visitations, and waiting "to greet death."[6]

But Valerian is hardly some kind of secular saint. Though in business he seems to lack the appetite for raw power, in his personal life he likes complete control. This desire for personal control can first be detected in how he shapes the natural environment to his own ends. The greenhouse he builds is meant as "a place of controlled ever-flowering life" (53). Ironically, it's more a place of death than life. Before Son comes in to literally shake them up, the flowers tend to stay closed and sag in the artificial air-conditioned climate. As for the island itself, Valerian has made it into a kind of false paradise by building a designer house safely removed from the intrusion of native life and by deliberately "adjusting the terrain for comfortable living" (53). When Valerian gets through, the place is rid of "rats, snakes and other destructive animal life" (53). In addition, trees have been cut down, the river has been redirected, and other land "development" completed. The place has been made to seem tame and safe, under control, just the way Valerian likes it.

Inside the house, everything seems under control, too. However, after Son arrives to shake the people in the house, like the flowers in the greenhouse, it becomes apparent just how much of a failure Valerian has actually been. During the Christmas meal, the news breaks that Valerian has fired Therese and Gideon, the natives who have worked on his place, for stealing apples. Ondine and Sidney erupt in bitterness, complaining that they should have been consulted. As the exchange between Valerian and his servants builds, all the rancorous feelings about being under Valerian's control during most of their lives emerge. Ondine also lets out the awful family secret that Margaret had physically abused Michael when he was a small child. Significantly enough, her sick action was ultimately directed at Valerian. As Ondine rightly concludes, Margaret "didn't stick pins in her baby. She stuck em in his baby. Her baby she loved" (279). Unfortunately for Michael, he served as a helpless surrogate for Valerian, against whose cold control Margaret was desperately trying to rebel.

In *Tar Baby*, just as in all her novels, the names Morrison chooses for her characters turn out to be quite appropriate. Named after a Roman emperor, Valerian has spent a lifetime acting like an unquestioned ruler. And as his last name additionally suggests, he has been accustomed to running over anything that might get in his way, people or land. But after he is confronted by the secret of Michael's abuse, his confident, powerful sense of himself shatters, and he literally begins to shake out of control. Seeing this happening, we may believe that he has learned the all-important lesson of letting go his oppressive grip. Morrison doesn't quite allow us to see in the text what Valerian finally thinks of his autocratic past. However, she does show Valerian ruminating over the most conclusive personal point, his crime of innocence.

In Morrison's world, choosing to be innocent is a great human flaw.[7] Her narrative voice makes this point more explicit in *Tar Baby* than in any other of her works. "An innocent man is a sin before God," we are told, "inhuman and therefore unworthy. No man should live without absorbing the sins of his kind, the foul air of his innocence" (243). This disturbing thought enters Valerian's mind as he finally realizes that his safe, controlled life has been shaken to its roots, and that it is time for him to confront his guilt directly. He now confesses to himself that he has been guilty of the kind of self-centered innocence that has let him "live with a woman who had made something kneel down in him the first time he saw her" but about whom he "knew nothing" because he has been too busy with himself. She had given him a son, but though he declared he loved him, he had to admit that he "knew nothing" about him either. It occurs to him after all this time that Michael, while he was being abused, might have sent out signals for help. But Valerian committed the "foul" crime of choosing to be innocent. The fact remains that he didn't know what was really going on in his house—whether it concerned his wife, his son, his servants, or his guests—because "he had not taken the trouble to know. He was satisfied with what he did know. Knowing more was inconvenient and frightening" (242).

He had been all his life preoccupied "with the construction of the world" to his own specifications, ignoring "the real message" his wife, his son, or anybody else under his rule might be trying to send him. Thus, concerning the oppressive influence or destructive effect he might have had on the world around him, all he could say in his defense was that "he did not know" (247). To his credit, though, Valerian in the end faces his guilt of innocence, and concludes with a rhetorical judgment: "Was there anything so loathsome as a willfully innocent man? Hardly" (243).

Margaret's story also arrives at a self-judgment. She has tried to play the beautiful innocent all her married life, but after the secret of Michael's abuse is revealed, she faces the split within her between an encouraged innocence and her true guilt. The morning after the secret comes out, she awakens from "the dream she ought to have had." The admiring looks of others had been her sustenance in life. Now, she rises with "the wonderful relief of public humiliation, the solid security of the pillory." Her face wears "that look of harmony" resulting from relieved discovery that the jig is up" (235). She has been caught, the world now knows that her attractive appearance has hidden great imperfections, and she feels glad.

As she considers what to do next, she decides that she really "had no idea." But because she now feels liberated from her formerly false, oppressive existence, she decides this was "not a problem to which she had to provide a solution. That was the future, her job at hand was to reveal the past" (235). In making this determination, she has started on the path toward the discovery that behind her victimization of her son was a history of her own victimization by the distorted needs of others. She had grown up as a poor girl who was first isolated because she didn't look like a member of her clan, and then she was admired for her breathtaking good looks rather than anything there might have been of value in her character. Aware of her attractiveness as a teenager, Margaret felt compelled to exploit it, although she evidently had no greater ambitions in life than to live in a safe little place with caring people. Whether she liked it or not, however, she embodied white America's myth of entrancing beauty. Thus, when Valerian first saw her, since he was himself an exponent of the American success myth, he had to have her. He might not have fully realized it, but he wanted her the more because she happened to have bright red hair and strikingly white skin, the same colors as the candy named for him. Taking Margaret as his wife when she was only seventeen, Valerian basically expected her to remain a kind of beauty queen who would reflect well on him. When Margaret discovered just how cold and lonely the life of a beautiful possession could be, she made overtures of friendship to Ondine. Valerian cut her off, however, because he thought it unseemly to "consort" with servants. Michael's birth helped only to a point, since he was also perceived as essentially "belonging" to Valerian. As the years passed, Margaret inevitably lost more and more of her simple longings for happiness, accepted the illusions of material safety instead, and finally surrendered to the false dream of physical beauty as an answer to her inner needs. She might have died a victim of this dream. Fortunately, Son arrives in time to help wake her up.

Like Margaret, Ondine and Sidney become victims of a false American dream. They have become prized servants whose lives are defined by their "belonging" to Valerian. Because Valerian is indeed a benevolent ruler, they let the years go by, passively accepting their condition just like Margaret. As their service time grows, they come to hold on to the illusion that they have become much more than servants to their master and that consequently they can safely work for him without surrendering control over their lives. Of course, the safety they have pursued has instead threatened to enslave them. Perhaps they are held in comfort, but they are "held" nevertheless, and they have paid a severe price in terms of their true identity. They refer to themselves as Philadelphia Negroes, extremely proud of their hard-working habits and contemptuous of anybody of their race who isn't like them. Thus, while Valerian welcomes Son to his dining table, they hate him intensely. They cannot think of this "swamp nigger" as a "Negro—meaning one of them" (107). Nor can they stand to think of Gideon and Therese as their racial kin, dismissing them as natives who don't even deserve to be called by their given names. They are just trash, generically referred to as "Yardman" and "Mary."

Sidney and Ondine have adopted the American dream of material safety, of personal dignity defined by a steady job. In the process, they have disavowed their roots and histories. Do they realize to what extent they have betrayed themselves? With Son's arrival, an opportunity for self-examination arises for everybody in Valerian's household. Valerian and Margaret are shaken awake, even if it would be going too far to claim that their stories have "happy" endings. It would be more correct to call their endings appropriately ironic, especially since Valerian becomes the "kept" person in the end. Additionally ironic is the fact that at the end he begins to resemble a "baby" who must depend on Sidney and Ondine. They now become in effect his "keepers," exchanging roles with him. This irony seems like a "happy" ending to them. But, of course, they are wrong.

Unfortunately for Sidney and Ondine, they never really awaken from their false dream. Margaret tells Valerian at one point that he need never worry about their ever leaving. "You couldn't pry them out of here. With or without Jade," she concludes. "They are yours for life" (31). How right she is. After the dust settles following the Christmas dinner explosion, it's clear that Sidney and Ondine haven't undergone any meaningful self-examination, and their main worry remains job security. Subsequently a significant exchange between Ondine and her niece takes place that seems to show an awakened heart. What Ondine has to say about the subject of being a good daughter is something Jadine needs to hear. Generally speaking, Ondine speaks with eloquent conviction of the need for loving connections between parent and child and the duties each has toward the other. However, the apparent integrity of her advice is undercut when later she and her husband express their main worry concerning Jadine. Would she bury them? They are afraid she won't, that they will have to depend on each other alone for a decent burial. A decent burial—this inevitably is their only remaining dream.

Sidney has a recurring dream that indicates most pointedly his self-betrayal and, by implication, the self-betrayal of his wife, too. In his dream, he is in his hometown of Baltimore. He remembers it as a "red city" turning "rust-colored." He had left Baltimore for Philadelphia, where he became "one of those industrious Philadelphia Negroes." Fifty years later his "most vivid dreams" are still of the place he left. "The fish, the trees, the music, the horses' harnesses"—a place quite different from respectable, staid, and bland Philadelphia. "It was a tiny dream he had each night that he would never recollect from morning to morning." Thus he "never knew what it was exactly that refreshed him" (61). If he would take the trouble to look inside himself, he would see what he had given up when he cut his roots. In Baltimore he may have been poor, but he was surrounded by the vivid, colorful life of his heritage. Now he was drowned in respectability, just like his wife, who also had a revealing dream defining her failed life. Ondine dreamed of "sliding into water, frightened that her heavy legs and swollen ankles will sink her" (61). They do, in fact, sink her, these legs and ankles swollen with respectable work, in the sense that her obsession with a decent end to her life has drowned the best qualities of her inherited blood.

The discussion thus far has dealt with four characters who hardly represent Morrison's ideal of life. Sidney and Ondine are basically set up as negative characters from whose mistakes one might learn. Although Valerian and Margaret are observed to make some estimable headway, they nevertheless remain marked by various imperfections. Thus, if there is a main character meant to represent Morrison's affirmative vision, it has to be either Jadine or Son. This apparently has been the thinking of most critics and general readers. And it is here that *Tar Baby* has been most often misread. The fact is that Morrison has written a deliberate cautionary tale. We are meant to learn from the *nega-*

tive examples of the main characters, all of whom are split with serious flaws. In the final analysis, we are particularly meant to learn from the examples of Jadine and Son, who between them actually contain Morrison's answer to a complete life for black Americans, but who are by themselves failures because they are pulled in different directions, winding up with dead-end dreams.

From the outside, Jadine looks enviable, like a queen with the world at her feet. By the age of twenty-five, she has "made it" in the Western commercial world. She is a graduate of the Sorbonne with the highest degree in art history. Her exceptional beauty has landed her a well-paying career in modeling. She has been discovered by the movies. And in Paris, where she has been living, handsome white men compete for her hand in marriage. What more could she want? The answer, simply put, is happiness. Something is missing in her life. What it is precisely she doesn't know. But Jadine suspects it has to do with an African woman she briefly sees in Paris while she shops at a grocery store for a dinner party organized to celebrate the latest fulfillment of her ambitions.

When the African woman walks into the grocery store, Jadine becomes spellbound. The woman is entirely regal and strikingly beautiful in a canary yellow dress that brings out the deep, tar-like blackness of her skin. Balancing three eggs in her hand, she walks out of the store, her many colored sandals seeming to leave gold tracks on the floor. Once outside, she turns around, looks directly at Jadine, who hasn't been able to take her eyes off her, and spits at her. Jadine tries to ignore the insulting gesture, but she can't quite get the woman and what she might mean out of her mind. She tries to convince herself that she was overreacting, that she should just forget about this woman. Like it or not, however, she continues to be deeply disturbed by the vision. Somehow the African woman has made her feel "lonely" and "inauthentic" (48).

The African woman is Morrison's most symbolic character in the novel. Clearly standing for an "authentic" black person neither culturally uprooted nor spoiled, she remains proudly a member of the tribe, which as far as Morrison is concerned is ultimately "the question." In Morrison's own words, this African woman was "the genuine article," a figure "invested with all the hopes and views of the person who observes her." What Jadine should see in her is "the original self—the self that

we betray when we lie, the one that is always there."[8] Unfortunately for Jadine, although haunted by this figure, in the end she
won't really learn to "see" and follow this "other" self which is
"authentic" and can show the whole way.[9]

Jadine is given a remarkable opportunity to rediscover her
"other" true self when Son arrives at Valerian's estate, where
Jadine seeks refuge from the haunting experience with the
African woman. Before she meets Son, however, she receives a
Christmas gift from her French fiance that forecasts her failure to
respond to this last, best chance for reassessing her life. The coat
he sends is made from "the hides of ninety baby seals stitched together so nicely you could not tell what part had sheltered their
cute little hearts and which has cushioned their skulls" (87). Instead of being revolted by this product of efficient commercial
slaughter, Jadine makes love to it. Sinking into its blackness, she
lay "spread-eagled on the fur, nestling herself into. It made her
tremble. She opened her lips and licked the fur. It made her
tremble more." There was "something fearful about the coat,"
she thinks. "No, not fearful, seductive" (112). Symbolically
speaking, then, she is seduced by this kind of dead black hide
when she should be choosing instead the black skin of the
African woman.

Right after this scene of material seduction, Son appears
in Jadine's bedroom. He will act as an inviting "black" alterna-
tive to her adopted "white" life. His function becomes immediately clear because, like the African woman, he is deliberately
depicted in symbolically suggestive terms during this crucial
scene. When Jadine decides to look at herself in a full-length
mirror to "judge the effect," a "smell hit her." At this moment
she becomes aware of a human presence in her bedroom.
She realizes that the smell is his "black smell" at the same time
she discovers Son's reflection in the mirror. His skin is "as
dark as a riverbed" and his hair looks "wild" and "over-
powering." She feels frightened and repulsed as she struggles
"to pull herself away from his image in the mirror" (113-14).
When he advances and takes her from behind, she resists
him—and by implication all he stands for. The fact that he
has earlier spent his nights as a fugitive trying "to insert his
own dream into her," and that he now tries "to breathe into her
the smell of tar and its shiny consistency," expresses clearly
enough the point that, while she has just been seduced by a
lifeless coat, he in turn tries to seduce her with his life-injecting

qualities that come from living a natural "black" life.

Although Jadine continues to struggle against his seductive influence, she responds to him, as Son himself notes, in the stereotypical fashion common to white girls. For a time, Son's seduction will appear to succeed. After the Christmas dinner debacle, they do sleep together, and they decide to stay together once they leave Valerian's place. But when they meet in New York, it quickly becomes apparent that their relationship is doomed. Jadine and Son still pull in opposite directions, split between loving and hating New York. "This is home," Jadine thought, "with an orphan's delight." It was a city full of competitive, decisive people "whose joints were oiled just like her" (222). By contrast, Son saw New York as a place where "black girls were crying," children were nowhere to be seen, and where "the street was choked with beautiful males who had found the whole business of being black and men at the same time too difficult and so they'd dumped it" (216). Following an interlude of love and fighting, Jadine agrees to take a trip with Son to his home town, Eloe, Florida. But there, against Son's hopes, the basic split between them widens rather than narrows. And Jadine soon makes her final decision to escape the attraction of *her* tar baby, meaning Son. She will subsequently board a plane bound for Paris and all the material promises of her adopted white culture. In the seat beside her will lie the seal skin coat, signifying that she has in the end chosen to wear the values it assumes instead of those assumed by Son.

Son will decide to pursue Jadine, but she is really a lost cause. Looking back at her story, it seems obvious enough that she was lost after she began to live under Valerian's sponsorship of her education. Since that time, she has grounded herself in her acquired culture so completely that she has cut herself off from her black roots. Severing her roots developed into a deliberate choice, a choice rather predictable for a "yalla," as far as Gideon is concerned. Gideon knows what he is talking about, having been in this world long enough to observe how hard it is for culturally confused blacks raised in a white world "not to be white people." These "yallas," as he calls them, "don't come to being black natural-like. They have to choose it and most don't choose it." (155).

Jadine comes away convinced that she has made the right choice of culture because it has given her the means to control her own life. She seems satisfied at the end that she no longer has to dream her life's dream because she has fulfilled it. She now controls the world she has wanted, she no longer has to strive for safety, she now feels "lean and male," and is sure that "she was the safety she longed for" (275, 290). Yet even as she looks forward to a life of self-control, she remains nagged by her split from Son. Despite her professed assurance, she asks herself: "What went wrong?" If she could hear Therese's opinion, she would know. Climaxing her case against Jadine, Therese tries to persuade Son to give her up because "she has forgotten her ancient properties" (290, 305). Son nevertheless still wants to catch Jadine. However, he must fail because, ironically enough, she is already caught by the "white" tar baby of materialism represented by the expensive seal coat.

In conventional social terms, Son is the least redeemable of characters. Although he has had some higher education, he is contemptuous of it as a means of personal and racial salvation. Admittedly a thief, he is also guilty of a more serious crime. Son killed his wife, however unintentionally, and then ran from the law. Drifting from job to job, he makes plain his intentions of never settling down to a regular work routine. He is, in short, a social rebel who consciously resists the system of industry adopted by Jadine. What follows is that there is too great a distance between Jadine and Son. This is underscored by a flash picture of Jadine's industrial patron and her outlaw lover facing off each other at the Christmas dinner table. Valerian, the patron "who respected industry looked over a gulf at the man who prized fraternity" (205). This gulf, unfortunately, seems precisely the kind destined to remain between Jadine and Son.

Referring to Son as a man who valued fraternity more than industry is just one indication that, whatever his social flaws, Morrison doesn't mean to offer him as unredeemable in the fundamental sense. On the contrary, she depicts him as someone who himself could serve at least as a partial redeemer of someone like Jadine. What she needs, and what Son represents in the final analysis, is not only the importance of fraternity but also the necessity of a kind of return to a more natural life. To emphasize the latter function, Morrison gives Son highly suggestive physical attributes. For example, he has "savannas in his face" (205). His smile is "like a sudden rustling of wind" (181). His voice sounds "woodsy" (181). His "smell" is an "animal" mustiness similar to the natural smell of earth (123). Of course, being called Son Green in itself expresses more emphatically than anything else his redeeming nature-bound values.

Beyond the values of fraternity and a natural life, Son also prizes the past. Morrison certainly sympathizes with this attribute, too. At the same time, however, she is realistic enough to know that clinging to the past can become yet another kind of tar baby that should be avoided. Son doesn't seem to know this, or if he does, he finds out too late. After the disastrous trip to Eloe, which in effect represents the past he clings to, he loses Jadine. In his desperation to get her back, he decides that he may have been wrong about the idyllic pictures of Eloe he has been carrying in his memory. Perhaps, he now thinks, Jadine was right all along in her arguments against Eloe and all he has defended. In actual fact, although Son is right to stop and think about his past, he is wrong to conclude that he might do best just to surrender to Jadine. He should indeed learn from her that one must be realistic enough to recognize one lives in *this* world, and this calls for certain adjustments. She, of course, should learn from him that one can't live a truly fulfilling life if one cuts the natural roots of one's communal past. Together, they could add up to answers to their problems. But unfortunately, as the final morpheme of the novel suggests, they are destined to "split."

* * * * * * * *

The fated split between Jadine and Son is highlighted by eruptions of dialectical arguments where both score sensible points. The problem is that they can't ever reach the required synthesis, and their individual arguments remain incomplete and inconclusive. These serious clashes intensify to an outright war after the trip to Eloe. As they begin to fight to the finish, neither gives ground. "Why do you want to *change* me?" asks Jadine. "Why do you want to change *me*?" he answers. Son mocks her for loving New York and for not really being "*from* anywhere." "I'm from Eloe," he says. Jadine shoots back: "I hate Eloe and Eloe hates me. Never was any feeling more mutual" (267).

Son's hatred for New York and all the material values it represents seems clear enough. A "natural" man, he is bound to despise the industrial world that, as far as he is concerned, teaches only one lesson well: "how to make waste" (203). New

York to him serves as an egregious example of the "defecating" modern world, and the last thing Son wants is to "*make* it" in such a place (267). Regarding Jadine's hatred of Eloe, the reason becomes especially clear when we recall her experience with the "night women."

When Jadine spends the night in Eloe, she has a nightmarish visitation. A crowd of women, materializing from the past and present, push in and gaze at her intently. "Cheyenne got in, and then the rest; Rosa and Therese and Son's dead mother and Sally Sarah Sadie Brown and Ondine and Soldier's wife Ellen and Francine from the mental institution and her own dead mother and even the woman in yellow." They "spoiled her lovemaking, taking away her sex like succubi." But not the sex of Son, who lay sleeping beside her undisturbed. Frightened and upset, Jadine whispers in a half voice: "What do you want with me, goddam it!" For an answer, they pull out their breasts. Deeply shocked, Jadine manages to respond plaintively: "I have breasts too." However, "they didn't believe her. They just held their own higher and pushed their own farther out and looked at her. All of them were revealing both their breasts except the woman in yellow. She did something more shocking—she stretched out a long arm and showed Jadine her three big eggs." Jadine becomes so frightened by this she begins to cry (259).

Especially because the African woman appears in this mystical scene, the view shared by most critics that "the night women represent a positive force" can't be denied.[10] But at the same time, the view should be qualified to a certain extent. In varying degrees, these women all doubtless represent the "authentic" qualities of personal and racial nurturing. They have the requisite "ancient properties" that continue to link them to their culture. And finally, each can be assumed to resemble the kind of daughter that Ondine in a later exchange specifically asks Jadine to be. "A daughter," Ondine tells her, "is a woman that cares about where she come from and takes care of them that took care of her." "What I want from you," she goes on, "is what I want for you. I don't want you to care about me for my sake. I want you to care about me for yours" (281). All this is the kind of advice Jadine surely needs to accept if she is going to be saved from a sterile, inauthentic life. Of course, it must at the same time be remembered that Ondine is herself sterile, and has in any case already been shown to lead a flawed

existence. What, then, must consequently be concluded? Jadine's response to Ondine that "there are other ways to be a
woman" seems to provide a satisfactory answer at first (281).
However, when she goes on to say that "your way is one . . . but
it's not my way," she expresses more directly than she realizes
both her own predicament and that of someone like Ondine.
The text, overall, argues that if there is "one way" to be a whole
black woman in the contemporary world, it requires "both" the
ways of the "night women" and of Jadine's kind of woman. To
put it another way, the text doesn't ask Jadine to stay in Eloe and
all it represents, but it does ask her to take with her and live with
the cultural lesson taught by the "night women" wherever she
might go. It is in this critical light that the "night women"
should indeed be seen as a positive force.

Jadine, however, sees the lesson of the "night women" in
only a negative way. She remains convinced that they were "all
out to get her, tie her, bind her. Grab the person she had worked
hard to become and choke it off with their soft loose tits" (267).
So, she runs away as quickly as she can. When Son rejoins her
in New York, they begin "the fight of their lives," with Jadine
knowing very well that she is ultimately "fighting the night
women," the black "mamas who had seduced him and were trying to lay claim to her" (267). Back and forth they now go, fling-
ing pointed words of disagreement at each other. Finally, their
struggle reaches a climax when Son attacks Jadine with his version of the tar baby tale. "Once upon a time there was a farmer—
a white farmer," he begins. "And he had this bullshit bullshit
bullshit farm. And a rabbit. A rabbit came along and ate a couple of his . . . ow . . . cabbages. . . . So he got this great idea about
how to get him. How to, to trap . . . this rabbit. And you know
what he did? He made him a tar baby. He made it, you hear
me? He made it" (270). Son of course sees himself as the rabbit
in this story, Jadine as the tar baby, and Valerian as the white
farmer.

Jadine responds to the pointed story with fury. She
doesn't see herself in the story's light, and she rejects the lesson
it implies about what she should do under the circumstances.
Son wants her to break from her past and choose his instead.
But Jadine has made up her mind to give him up at last. Thus
she tells him conclusively: "You stay in that medieval slave bas-
ket if you want to. You will stay there by yourself. Don't ask me
to do it with you. I won't. There is nothing any of us can do

about the past but make our own lives better, that's all I've been trying to help you do. That is the only revenge, for us to get over. *Way* over. But no . . . you don't know how to forget the past and do better" (271). And so, far apart in their views, their doomed affair ends.

Morrison once said that the structure of *Tar Baby* is to some extent modeled on "the sort of call-and-response thing" found in "peasant stories" where "the narrator functions as the chorus." Since such stories "don't pass any judgments" directly, neither does Morrison in her novel.[11] Still, the recipients of such a story must be given grounds for sound judgments themselves. The sides of the issues at stake must certainly be clear. In such stories, this responsibility is traditionally left up to a choral narrator. Thus in *Tar Baby*, as the struggle between Jadine and Son reaches a climax, Morrison brings in a narrator for the following summarizing passage, a passage that perfectly expresses the thematic split embodied by the doomed lovers: "Each was pulling the other away from the maw of hell—its very ridge top. Each knew the world as it was meant or ought to be. One had a past, the other a future and each one bore the culture to save the race in his hands. Mama-spoiled black man, will you mature with me? Culture bearing black woman, whose culture are you bearing?" (269). Responsive readers of Morrison's whole text are bound to make the judgment that the characters must be both "mature" and "culture bearing" or they are lost.

* * * * * * * *

Tar Baby is made up of an amazing mixture. A serious book, it also has a comic and sometimes even absurdist quality. The style is in turn polished and vulgar, elegiac and violent, poetic and dramatically functional. The language of the uneducated appears in one place, the language of sophisticated literature in another, complete with literary allusions and symbolic imagery of all kinds. For folklore and mythology, both African and Western cultures serve as sources. Running throughout is a kind of parody of the original Christmas story. The protagonists, all of them split in two by their failed lives, multiply into paradoxical clashes. Various other examples could be cited. But what should be pointed out in any event is that none of this happened in an unmindful way. Morrison herself knew very well that while she was writing the novel she was putting together "bits and pieces."[12]

As has already been mentioned, there are some critics who have rightly complained that *Tar Baby* has at times a rather disjointed quality. True, the "bits and pieces" don't always hold together perfectly. In the final analysis, however, Morrison succeeds by and large in pulling together this complex novel that she herself once described as "really kind of crazy."[13] The "craziest" thing about the novel, and at the same time the most significant means of holding the parts together, is her extraordinary use of nature.

On the whole, nature acts like an additional character in the story, as complicated and important as a human protagonist.[14] Thus, for example, the animal life can observe, react, and comment on the action. The rivers are capable of the deepest emotions. Trees can be seductive as a lover. Ants can marshal campaigns, and swamps can grasp like rapists. This general anthropomorphizing of nature had its risks, Morrison surely knew. There might be some Western critics who would accuse her of falling into the trap of pathetic fallacy. As a matter of fact, this is precisely what happened.[15] Nevertheless, she could hope that the ultimate point of her strategy would be discovered, the point in keeping with her ambition to write more in the African than the Western vein. In the African vein, nature is *fully* alive, meaning that it is not materially separated from human existence. This basic fact explains Morrison's decision to personalize nature. But additionally, she hoped that the nature she depicted would also reflectively emphasize her concern with the issue of the material world at odds with the natural. With its living presence in *Tar Baby*, nature implies the extra factor needed to heal unnatural human division. Beyond that, nature serves as a stylistic correlative, helping to unify the story's "bits and pieces" into a whole.

Finally, Morrison joined an involved nature with the framing device of a prologue and an epilogue to provide her story with a further sense of wholeness. In the prologue, Son is swimming toward the island when the ammonia scented water grabs him and, "like the hand of an insistent woman," pushes him and urges him in a rhythm resembling birth. In the epilogue, he again moves through water toward the island, his passage again like a birth. A primary difference is that in the prologue Son is actually urged by the water away from the shore, while in the epilogue he is urged forward. At the novel's end,

Son is pictured standing up and running straight ahead, "looking neither to the left nor to the right," as if he knows where he is going (306).

This ending seems rather ambivalent, and so some critical controversy surrounded it. On one side of the debate the ending has been called nothing less than a "muddle."[16] On another side, it has been called an "optimistic" picture of Son's final success as a man.[17] While critics have continued the argument, Morrison herself has provided the clearest answer to the question of her final intention. What she wanted was "to suggest that this journey is Son's choice—although he did not think it up, Therese did. He said he had no choice, so she manipulated his trip so that he had a choice. On his way back to Valerian's house . . . there is a strong possibility that he joins or is captured by the horsemen captured by the past, by the wish, by the prehistoric times. The suggestion in the end, when the trees step back to make way for a certain kind of man, is that Nature is urging him to join them. First he crawls, then he stands up, he stumbles, then he walks, and last, he runs, and his run is lickety-split, lickety-split, which has a movement of some confidence, and also suggests the beat of a rabbit running."[18] Therefore, Son apparently becomes one with the past and with nature, which all along he was meant to embody. But saying this ending is clear because it was inevitable isn't the same as saying it's a happy one. Morrison on one occasion declared that while writing *Tar Baby* she had "wished" for a happy ending.[19] The realist in her, however, knew that Son's natural primitivism was not the final way out of an incomplete life, any more than was Jadine's way. A consummate equation would have added Son's reverence for the past to Jadine' eagerness for the future, both joined by the presence of a living nature. But *Tar Baby* cannot end with such an ideal equation because it aspires to be a story providing admonishing examples of unnatural entrapment and human separation.

Chapter 6

Trilogy in Progress:
Beloved and *Jazz*

After *Beloved* was published, Morrison felt sure that this, her fifth novel, would be the least read of her writings. Who could imagine people rushing out to buy a book on the horrors of slavery in America? She herself admits to having had a great reluctance to dwell on a subject that would force her to focus on the most painful period in her people's history. She knew that recalling the slave era would be a heart-wrenching experience for her on a very personal level. Nevertheless, she felt a compulsion to write the story because it had to be told. No one had yet told the *real* story; it seemed no one even wanted to think about the subject in a serious way. Morrison sensed a "national amnesia" surrounding the details of slavery and its aftermath. Not the blacks, not the whites wanted to remember. Significantly, not even the characters she would create for *Beloved* wanted to remember.[1] The task she set for herself, then, ran the risk of her writing a book that would be shunned. But to Morrison's surprise, *Beloved* became a best seller that garnered her not only a great deal of critical praise but also a wider readership than she had ever hoped for.

The genesis of the novel goes back to the time when Morrison was working on black literature projects for Random House. While editing *The Black Book*, a collection of items about the struggle of African-Americans over the course of 300 years, she came across a number of stories about slaves who dared to resist the system. One in particular caught her eye. This was the story of Margaret Garner, a fugitive who had escaped with her children from Kentucky and settled in a neighborhood just outside Cincinnati. When pursued and threatened with re-enslavement, she resisted by trying to kill her own children. Garner succeeded in taking the life of one, making the point that she would go even to this length to avoid seeing her children forced back into slavery. Although Morrison didn't include this particular story in *The Black Book*, it stayed with her and eventually grew into an obsessive memory that became the germ for *Beloved*.[2] However, it didn't become clear to her that the story she had read was growing into a novel in her imagination until she came across another story and a picture contained in *The Harlem Book of the Dead*. The story which struck her this time centered on a young woman shot in a crowd of dancers, apparently by a jealous boyfriend. Only she knew who had done it. Before dying, she was pressed to identify her assailant, but she refused to say anything until "tomorrow" so he would have time to get away. Following the fashion of that time, the "beloved" young woman was photographed lying in a coffin, beautifully dressed. Morrison recalls that after reading this story, and seeing the accompanying picture, something "connected" for her. She still can't say exactly what made these stories snap together in her imagination, but she does know that in both instances she was seeing remarkable examples of how much a woman could love in a sacrificial way, of how a woman could place the value of her life in something other than herself.[3] Whatever else these stories might have said, to Morrison they ultimately provided "noble" ideas around which to build *Beloved* and *Jazz*, the first two novels of her projected trilogy meant to cover the whole story of African-Americans.

Beloved is based on a great deal more active research than is usual in Morrison's "poetic" kind of fiction. The book is dedicated to "sixty million and more." This figure refers to the estimated number of Africans rounded up for the slave trade who either died while awaiting transportation or who died during the passage on the slave ships. Although this figure is not the only estimate available, it represents the most reliable educated guess that Morrison could find. The fact that this figure remains a guess says something important about what Morrison was up against in trying to find out the full story of the slave trade. Much of that story has been ignored, left behind, or simply lost. When she went to various slave museums, for example, she found them of little help. They contained examples of the handiwork of the slaves. But where were the chains and restraining mechanisms? She discovered that if she wanted to see these devices, she would have to go to Brazil because none of the American slave museums displayed them. She searched in folklore and songs for any useful information, but found "a big blank." She went through the pertinent historical writings and the slave narratives published in this country. However, there was a dearth of useful historical writing. And in the case of the slave narratives, she was very disappointed to find that they hardly told the full, ugly truth because they were adjusted for nineteenth-century abolitionist readers. The writers of these narratives pulled back whenever the facts became too shocking or painful, afraid they might upset their sympathetic white readers and thus lose their support. What most disappointed Morrison about slave narratives, however, was the fact that "there was no mention of their interior life."[4] This is where Morrison's imagination stepped in, and indeed took over.

Because *Beloved* is ultimately a work of sustained imagination, it would be imprecise to label it a historical novel, as so many critics have tried to do. Although a great deal of research does stand behind the writing, it has been so fully assimilated into Morrison's imagination that any historical "facts" lie buried in the text as necessary, natural parts of the story. Morrison says that while she did consciously use some researched material, it was not in a documentary way. Rather, she used such material to make her characters "narrow and deep." During the actual process of writing this story, she was careful to tell herself that she was, as always, primarily concerned with individual people and their interior lives. This was not a book "about the institution—Slavery with a capital S. It was about these anonymous people called slaves. What they do to keep on, how they make a life, what they're willing to risk, however long it lasts, in order to relate to one another."[5] Thus in keeping with her design to make her novel a "personal" experience, she deliberately avoided learning more than "the obvious stuff" about Margaret Garner, lest the "facts" got in the way of her imagination. "I wanted to invent her life," Morrison says, because "I wanted to be accessible to anything the characters had to say about it" and be "available to anything that might be pertinent."[6]

Morrison says that when she actually started writing the story, she meant it to be "about the feeling of self" women express best "through nurturing." For Morrison, the central question in the case of Margaret Garner's story was how and why that nurturing instinct could lead to infanticide.[7] This kind of issue posed "a lot of danger" for her, she recalls. She was deeply aware of the "responsibility" she owed her protagonist and the history behind her.[8] She felt she had to provide the "inner" truth about all of these victims of slavery, so that, in a manner of speaking, all those "unburied or at least unceremoniously buried" people could finally be "properly, artistically" placed to rest. Of course, in the case of someone like Margaret Garner, the responsibility to tell the "inner" truth was complicated by the issue of guilt. Thus Morrison knew that in her novel her protagonist, whose story is drawn from the story of Margaret Garner, would ultimately have to be judged for her ferocious action. Since she wasn't "there" Morrison felt she couldn't be this necessary "judge," and as the book developed she came to feel that nobody else who knew the woman could adequately play this role either. That is, there was nobody else alive who could play this role. Thus it occurred to Morrison that the murdered child was the only possibility left. And this was how the "ghostly" character, Beloved, "inserted herself into the text."[9]

On the surface, *Beloved* might be read as a ghost story. The story takes place during the years surrounding the Civil War, and it revolves around Sethe, the character inspired by Margaret Garner. Because of her act of infanticide, Sethe has been ostracized by the community, and so she has withdrawn into a stoical, isolated existence shared by her remaining daughter and, apparently, by a ghost that haunts the house they live in. When the action of the novel begins, it has been many years since Sethe killed her other daughter to prevent re-enslavement. During this interim, her mother-in-law has died, the person in Sethe's life who came closer than anyone in being able to embrace Sethe's inner agony. And Sethe's other two children, both boys, have run off in fright. They couldn't shake the memory of their mother's planning to kill all her children, and they couldn't deal with the signs of a spiteful ghost living in the house, a ghost all the occupants seem to accept as the returned spirit of the baby daughter Sethe killed.

Then a character named Paul D. arrives on the scene. He knows Sethe from a time when they were slaves together at Sweet Home, the plantation from which Sethe has escaped. Their reunion promises to bring real love into the haunted house. But after Paul D. apparently drives out the malicious spirit ruling in the house, another figure arrives and begins to possess the house and its inhabitants. This is the title character, a mysterious, strangely child-like young woman of untold origins who does not explain herself clearly. Sethe's daughter, Denver, soon concludes that this is surely the murdered infant returned from the dead. Sethe will reach the same conclusion. So will others in the story. And apparently so have most readers, if the reviews and critical comments following the novel's publication are any indication.[10]

The readers who believe that the character called Beloved must be "the ghost become flesh," as one critic puts it, are certainly not entirely wrong.[11] After all, the fact that various characters in the novel come to this conclusion should be taken into account. But what must be further taken into account is that Morrison's "ghostly" creation is far too complex to be pinned down so directly, or to be pinned down at all in a final, materially defining sense. Like a true spirit, this character remains elusive, embodying certain ideas and functions, embodying not just herself literally but also metaphorically, and always ambiguously. Of course, the way she is ambiguously presented in the text must serve Morrison's subjective intents or we would merely have technique and trickery. What were Morrison's intents for this character? There were primarily two. Morrison meant for Beloved to be a kind of "mirror" character who would reflect the inner lives of the characters with whom she made contact. Thus in the case of Sethe, Beloved would act to reflect the mother's fears and hopes surrounding the killing of her baby daughter. The other primary intent for Beloved had to do with Morrison's deep sense of responsibility with regard to telling the story of her people's slavery as fully and honestly as possible. Thus, Beloved is also meant to be taken as a character reflecting the real experience of native Africans who lived through the Middle Passage. By means of this double intent designed for Beloved, Morrison hoped, as she says, to bridge "the gap between Africa and Afro-America and the gap between the living and the dead and the gap between the past and the present."[12]

Whenever Beloved appears in the text, then, she should always be read on more than one level, basically on two. On one hand, she is a ghost; but she is a ghost more in a thematic than an actual way. That is, she behaves with complete consistency like a haunting spirit—to those prepared to be haunted while they are driven by guilt feelings or desires. Thus, Sethe comes to the (undeniable) conclusion that her dead daughter has returned to haunt her guilty conscience, and Denver comes to believe that her dead sister has reappeared in response to her own yearnings for reunion. Nevertheless, while Beloved becomes a ghost for these and other characters in the story, she is meant at the same time to be taken as an actual survivor from a slave ship.[13] In this sense, she is flesh, a human being with her own horrifying story to tell. As a traumatized victim, Beloved remains incapable of telling her story except in painful bits and pieces. But these fragments are worked into the text in such a way that what she tells Sethe and Denver and what they think she says are two different things—and yet the same. They are finally the same in that while Beloved talks about one death (the Middle Passage), Sethe and Denver think of another (the infant's death), and thus use the same death-inspired language. And because they use the same language while speaking of two different death experiences, these experiences overlap and, in the final analysis, merge in the text into a general, summarizing statement that the death of Sethe's child and the "death" the young woman experienced through the Middle Passage have the same root cause of slavery, both being inseparable parts of the whole story of slavery and the memory of the enslaved.

This memory of the enslaved is, of course, carried by all the characters in *Beloved* who suffered under the system. Understandably, they would just as soon not bear this memory because it is such a painful burden. They would like to forget, if they could, and live in the present, which happens to be several years after emancipation. But they musn't forget, so the novel argues. They must remember and pass on their stories. Otherwise, they will have suppressed an essential part of their being, and not incidentally an essential part of history. They must be willing to look back on their past experiences, however dreadful those might have been, so that a kind of purging, cathartic recovery can occur, a process of recovery ending in a fuller self-realization and a discovery of personal worth. It is then that these characters can feel truly free, escape their death-like obsessions, and reclaim their lives.

The process of memory is naturally complicated, especially when there is a powerful reluctance to remember. This fact explains why *Beloved* is composed in the way it is. The novel moves back and forth between the present and the past, between the unfolding action and the recollections set in motion by the clash of characters and events. Gradually, step by fragmentary step, the full stories of the central characters form themselves. All along, the involved characters show their reluctance to remember by using strategies of avoidance mirrored in the structure of the text. Most notably, like the text, they tend to circle around the most painful memories, facing them only after undergoing intense experiences of reflection, which are expressed in the text primarily by certain metaphoric set pieces and interior monologues. In the end, looking back at the method of composition, it becomes clear that Morrison's purpose, as always, was to join the style to the subject matter as closely as possible. The unsettling and involved style reflects the disturbingly touching stories of the enslaved.

* * * * * * * *

The main challenge and hope that Morrison holds out for her characters (and her readers) is that they will recall the past and dare to confront it, however traumatic it may have been. Suppressing the past may help her characters survive, but it doesn't allow for authentic life. Suppressing the past results in another form of enslavement, holding the inner life captive to recurring fears and possibly neurotic obsessions. This lesson is repeated quite systematically in *Beloved*, in the sense that the central characters' stories move toward this conclusion. At least such a case can be made when the stories of Sethe and Paul D. are reviewed, and perhaps to a less obvious extent when the stories of Baby Suggs and Denver are likewise reviewed. Beloved's ambiguous case is similar, but necessarily only up to a point, since by her ambiguous nature and special function her story has to end in a rather open-ended fashion.

In African lore there are certain river spirits, seeming lunatics, believed to have contact with the unseen world. They are primarily identified by something strange about their hands and feet.[14] The young woman who suddenly appears and assumes the title role in the novel has hands and feet with unnaturally smooth and soft skin that looks "new." She arrives by rising from a river, makes Sethe's bladder break with a flood remindful of all the water that had come with the birth of Denver, and gulps down cup after cup of water "as though she had crossed a desert."[15] "You from around here?" asks Sethe. No, she shakes her head. "What might your name be?" asks Paul D. "Beloved," she says, in such a low and rough voice that "each one looked at the other two" (52). With the help of various suggestive signs, what they come to "see" in each other is the key to their own stories. Sethe is prepared to "see" her dead daughter, and so she sees her in Beloved, helped along by the fact that Beloved is the one word that she had put on her dead daughter's gravestone. Paul D. is prepared to "see" a young woman "drifting from ruin," prompted by the fact that he could identify with such an existence.   Later, Denver comes to "see" her dead sister in Beloved because of her own need to break out of a stultifying loneliness. Beloved herself looks hungrily at Sethe, hovering "like a familiar" around her (57).

What we eventually learn about Beloved is that in Sethe she "sees" a reflection herself, and also her deepest wish, to re-join *her* mother. Beloved's mother is herself a "ghostly" figure, apprehended in ambiguous bits and pieces. Toward the end of the novel, Morrison provides a series of internal monologues by Sethe, Denver, and Beloved, allowing us to hear them describe their possessive relationship to their "ghostly" other. And in Beloved's case, we are also allowed to see a picture, however fractured, reflecting her African past and the slave ship experi-ence. Elsewhere in the text, there are allusions to the possibility that after her arrival in this country, she became a confined sex-ual slave to some white men. When she disappears toward the end of the novel, she is evidently pregnant. The last reported glimpse of her is of a naked woman running through the woods. Looking as if she had "fish for hair," she was apparently aiming to return to the river from which she had first emerged (267). In other words, she looks more like an African water spirit than an actual human being. What are we to conclude, then? Is she a person or a spirit? It is a credit to Morrison's stylistic virtuosity that both views are possible and, thematically speaking, even necessary. In the end, Beloved embodies the "ghost" of slavery that *must* haunt both personal and historical memories.

When we are first introduced to Sethe, we learn that "she worked hard to remember as close to nothing as was safe" (6). Then Paul D. walks back into her life, and before long Beloved follows. Between them they force Sethe to think about her past existence, including her most painful memories. Paul D.'s pres-ence forces her to review her life as a slave, especially while at Sweet Home. This plantation, run by a benevolent couple, was an extraordinarily beautiful place. But its edenic appearance fails to cover up the fact that it can suddenly turn into a hell for the enslaved. When the plantation owner dies and his wife comes down with a cancerous illness, the conditions for Sethe and the rest of the slaves change drastically. The job of running the plantation is assumed by a man who believes the slave system both rational and just, because to him slaves are literally animals. Thus, life for the slaves at Sweet Home turns increasingly harsh and cruel, with the result that they plan to escape north. The plan, however, only partially succeeds. Sethe manages to get her children out, and she herself makes her escape, even though pregnant with Denver. Her husband, however, fails to make it, along with Paul D. and others. Deep inside, she knows that those left behind must have faced atrocities, as she did herself. When Paul D. begins to recall some of these atrocities, Sethe thinks to herself: "I don't want to know or have to remember that" (70).

Sethe's resolve on the "serious work of beating back the past" is weakened after Paul D.'s reappearance (73). But it takes the presence of Beloved to break down her resolve to the point where she can confront the most disturbing parts of her past. Once she comes to believe that Beloved is her lost daughter, she feels relieved of the burden of memory. "I don't have to remember nothing," Sethe thinks to herself. "I don't even have to explain. She understands it all" (187). Feeling that here indeed is someone who can understand allows Sethe voluntarily to recall the death scene of her daughter. It allows her also to recall such painful memories as the disappearance of her husband, the loss of her two sons, and the death of Baby Suggs. Finally, it allows her to tell for the first time her most humiliating experience at Sweet Home. This was her discovery that she was being studied as a creature with human characteristics listed on one side and animal characteristics on the other. It was this experience that weighed more than any other behind her decisions first to escape with her children from the plantation and then to kill her children rather than see them return to slavery.

Beloved's presence has a positive influence on Sethe up to this point, but beyond that she turns out to have a destructive effect. She becomes a possessive presence feeding on Sethe's "thick" love. Sethe becomes obsessed with pleasing Beloved, so that she can make up to her and reclaim her love. Beloved responds by driving Paul D. out of the house, appropriately enough by offering herself to his animal lust. In the case of Denver, Beloved increasingly holds her affection in thrall. Finally, with reference to Sethe, she begins to imitate her and almost replaces her while Sethe at the same time begins to resemble Beloved. The point of this near exchange of places and personalities is that Beloved becomes a kind of metaphoric incubus that feeds on Sethe's guilt feelings and "thick" maternal love. As a result, Sethe becomes a slave again, this time to a consuming love threatening her well-being just as much as the emotional death slavery brought. Once again, Sethe is in danger of slipping into a kind of self-contempt that the institution of slavery encouraged in its victims. To free herself from the bondage of past and present enslavement, Sethe must accept the lesson of love Baby Suggs tried to pass on. "Here," Baby Suggs preached, "in this place, we flesh; flesh that weeps, laughs; flesh that dances on bare feet in grass. Love it. Love it hard. Yonder they do not love your flesh. They despise it. They don't love your eyes; they'd just as soon pick em out. No more do they love the skin on your back. Yonder they flay it. And O my people they do not love your hands. Those they only use, tie, bind, chop off and leave empty. Love your hands! Love them. Raise them up and kiss them. Touch others with them, pat them together, stroke them on your face 'cause they don't love that either. *You* got to love it, *you*!" Baby Suggs continues in this vein, urging her listeners to love all parts of their bodies. She ends her sermon by stressing the importance of loving above all the heart. "Love that too," she cries out. "More than eyes or feet. More than lungs that have yet to draw free air. More than your life-holding womb and your life-giving private part, hear me now, love your heart. For this is the prize" (88-89).

Sethe can accept this lesson of love completely in the end, but she has to have the help of people who themselves have undergone the process of reclaiming their hearts. Denver escapes from the emotionally enslaving house so that she can return to it as a benefactor. A community of women, who had kept their distance out of spite and resentment inspired by Sethe's apparent pride, returns to the haunted house like a Greek chorus to help drive out the consuming spirit. Sethe withdraws from any help, however, after she tries to kill the white abolitionist who has befriended her family. She thinks, feverishly, that when Mr. Bodwin arrives to give Denver a lift to work, he looks like one of those other white men from many years ago who had come to the house for her and her children. The confusion in her mind may seem mad, but on second thought, it suggests a certain important logic. Sethe "recognizes" that a white man, even the most benevolent, continues to represent the threat of a system where her position in life is decided by skin color. When she tried to fight this system before, she wound up acting in a desperately defensive way that almost led to self-destruction. Now, however, she is impelled to rush at the white man, not away into hiding as before, in order to fight him directly. Of course, such directly aggressive behavior isn't meant to be taken as a final solution to Sethe's problem. Sethe in fact seems to give up on life after this episode. Still, it must be remembered that Beloved "this time" manages to run off while her "mother" fights for her with heart-felt passion.

The crucial irony of this scene underscores Sethe's misdirected and confused love. Beloved, after all, may be just a stranger who wound up staying with her. On the other hand, it might be less disturbing if she were just a stranger. To the community of black women who come to exorcise Beloved from Sethe's house, she looks like a "devil-child." She may be that and more. These women are frightened by her, but they are at the same time spellbound by the vision of a beautiful pregnant woman, "naked and smiling," with "vines of hair twisted all over her head. Jesus" (261). What is she, a runaway, a devil, or a goddess? Morrison, of course, means to keep an ambiguous balance allowing for all these possibilities. But whatever else she has been or may be, for Sethe she has become a destroyer. This is why, despite what Sethe thinks, her disappearance becomes the most fortunate development because it frees Sethe from a constant reflection of her guilt and from being entirely possessed by her past. Guilt and the past must not be avoided. They must be taken up and possessed. In a way, though, the reverse has finally happened to Sethe. She has been possessed by guilt and the past. And this fact very nearly destroys her. After the disappearance of Beloved, no longer "possessed" by her presence, Sethe is at long last prepared for the final lesson that will lead her to authentic re-birth, a lesson brought by Paul D. At the end of the story, Paul D. once more walks back into Sethe's life. Sethe bemoans the loss of Beloved. "She was my best thing," she says. Paul D. answers, "You your best thing, Sethe. You are." With Paul D.'s fingers holding hers, she questions, "Me? Me?" (272-273). The answer, which we can fill in, is: Yes, Paul D. is right when he implies that Sethe must recognize that only if she begins with love of self can she finish her journey to true freedom and a free love of life.

When Paul D. returns to Sethe, she correctly senses that he "wants to put his story next to hers" (273). In doing so, he also will be able to finish his journey out of enslavement. With his help, Sethe has come to the point where she can reclaim her life and love life again. Paul D. now sees in turn that Sethe is a woman who can "gather" him into a whole, take the "pieces" that he is and "gather them and give them back . . . in all the right order" (272-73). With her help, he can give up "the serious work of beating back the past" and, like Sethe, open up his heart to the possibilities of living and loving like a truly free and whole human being.

When Paul D. first walks back into Sethe's life, he knows that he has a "tobacco tin buried in his chest where a red heart used to be. Its lid rusted shut." And he doesn't intend to pry it open because "if she got a whiff of the contents it would shame him" (72-73). The contents of his heart have the smell of death-like fear. But this is no wonder. Paul D.'s story is like a case history of how far the degradation of slaves could go. When caught trying to escape from Sweet Home, he is treated like a dangerous beast. A bit is placed in his mouth, a spiked metal collar around his neck, and shackles around his feet. Then, tied to a buck-board, he is led off to be sold. As he leaves the plantation, his head brims with dreadful thoughts of what has happened to the other slaves involved in the escape plan. Then he sees Mister, the main rooster on the place. "I swear he smiled," he tells Sethe. To Paul D. the rooster looked "Better than me. Stronger, tougher. Son of a bitch couldn't even get out of the shell by his-self but he was still king and I was. . . ." Paul D. can't bring him-self to say exactly what he was, but he certainly knows that he was something "less than a chicken in the sun of a tub." Of course, that was because the rooster "looked so . . . free" (72).

After Paul D. tries to free himself by attempting to kill his new owner, he is sent to Georgia to become part of a chain gang. Here, he undergoes the most brutal and dehumanizing treatment. He is caged in a cell that was "a grave calling itself quarters" (106). White guards treat him, like all the other prisoners, in the most demeaning and violent way imaginable. Thus his human heart begins to die. "Life was dead" (109). Only a rainfall of biblical proportions allows him a miraculous escape. Then his years of running and wandering all over the country begin. During these years, he is mostly "free," but not in the fullest sense. On occasion he will literally walk back into various kinds of captivity. He will always break away, but it appears he will never reach that "safe" place where he will feel he can stop, that is, until he walks to Sethe's house. "When I got here," he tells Sethe, "and sat out there on the porch, waiting for you, well, I knew it wasn't the place I was heading toward; it was you." His heart begins to beat with love again, and he tells her, "We can make a life, girl. A life" (46).

To make that life, Paul D. will have to share his full life, including the painful past. This is where Beloved again plays her haunting role. When Paul D. first sees Beloved, he thinks, "I didn't want to be nowhere around her. Something funny about her. . . . She reminds me of something. Something, look like, I'm supposed to remember" (234). Yes, he is supposed to remember all that Beloved embodies as a "ghost" of slavery's full story. Only after Paul D. can assimilate his personal story with the wider story of his people can he come to Sethe with the desire to place his story next to hers; and only then can he finally know that the most sinister effect of slavery was the injection of self-contempt, which had to be countered by an insistent recognition of self-worth. The demeaning experiences of enslavement brought almost complete death to his heart; but partly because of the disturbing influence of Beloved, he senses that he might be one of the beloved himself, and thus could truly love another.

Of all the painful stories found in *Beloved*, the story of Baby Suggs is the saddest. Evidently a survivor of the Middle Passage, she lives for many years as a slave on different places, giving birth to a series of children by various men. Only when she arrives at Sweet Home does the brutal existence soften to any real extent. Here, she is actually allowed to live with her son, Halle, her only child not taken from her at an early age. After sixty years of slavery, Baby Suggs crosses the Ohio River as a free woman. Working constantly, her son has managed to purchase her freedom. Suddenly, she looks at her hands and is dazed by a clear recognition: "These hands belong to me. These *my* hands." Then she "felt a knocking in her chest and discovered something else new: her own heart beat" (141). Having reclaimed her heart, she sets out to use it in a loving way. She becomes "Baby Suggs, holy," dedicating her heart with loving energy to the welfare of others. But her great heart breaks after Sethe's act of infanticide and the subsequent spiteful withdrawal of the black community she has served with dedication.

Baby Suggs had preached the lesson that Sethe, Paul D., and everybody else in the black community had to learn in order to become truly free. She had preached that "The only grace they could have was the grace they could imagine" (88). What she counseled was that they could only be saved by starting to love themselves, in the flesh. She delivered this lesson of salvation with such complete conviction that, when Sethe killed her own flesh out of desperation, Baby Suggs dismissed all the hope she had been preaching. "Those white things have taken all I had or dreamed," she concluded, "and broke my heartstrings too. There is no bad luck in the world but whitefolks." And so she retreated from the world and spent her last days contemplating the colors of life besides whiteness, believing that "she had not lied. There was no grace—imaginary or real" (89). But actually Baby Suggs *had* told the truth about self-love as a source of grace. Where she had gone wrong was in also believing that her people should put their painful past away, once and for all. Her advice on the surface sounded wise. "Lay em down. . . . Sword and shield" (86). This is what Baby Suggs had done. But when the moment of crisis arrived, when the white world pursued Sethe and her family, and Baby Suggs could only stand by helplessly, she couldn't forget how this experience clashed with her professed dreams and beliefs. If haunted by this experience, Baby Suggs is actually being affected in the way she should. But she ends by trying mightily to suppress the memory, whereas she should be drawing on the killing scene, a response that could have strengthened her within. Sadly enough, she fails to realize this and "her faith, her love, her imagination and her great big old heart began to collapse" (89).

Of Baby Suggs' generation, the character who reflects most closely her experiences and desires is Stamp Paid. After he gained his freedom his heart also began to beat with an embracing love to do good for others. As his name suggests, however, he never forgets the price he has been forced to pay as a slave. While still a slave, his name was Joshua. But he changed it after an extreme experience of emasculation. His wife was taken as a concubine by the master of the plantation. He was first tempted by murderous thoughts, then decided instead to "free" himself. He would do this by remembering always what slavery had cost him, draw a line under this cost, and then take possession of his own life. Calling himself Stamp Paid indicated precisely this. He had paid all he was going to pay; he was free of a debt to "that" society. With this sense of being free, he found himself inspired by the same kind of love that Baby Suggs had experienced when she crossed into freedom. In the case of Stamp Paid, however, his energizing feeling of generous love never stopped, even though he could get "bonetired" just like Baby Suggs (76). She withdrew her caring heart when "the whitefolks had tired her out at last" (180). Stamp Paid continues the sacrificial struggle. Drawing upon the strength his name signifies, he dares to deal with the variety of "ghosts" haunting his community.

Coincidentally, in his role as a kind of community redeemer, it is Stamp Paid who saves Denver from being killed by Sethe, along with her sister. Thus, he has a special feeling for her from the start. After Beloved disappears from Sethe's house, Stamp Paid's satisfaction in his having saved Denver grows. When he says of her, "That's my heart," he is closer to the truth than he realizes (265). Denver, it seems, turns out to have a big, courageous heart like the one that beats in Stamp Paid. And of course he is right when he further says of her: "She turned out fine. Fine" (266). He draws this conclusion when he recalls that it was Denver who first wrestled her mother down before she could murder Mr. Bodwin. After this episode, Sethe collapses into a state resembling the final, defeated one of Baby Suggs. But Denver works to rescue them both. She manages to do this by daring to keep the past in mind, drawing a line under it, and then looking into the future in which she can care for others because she has learned to care for herself. Not long ago, Denver couldn't imagine ever leaving Sethe's house, her mother, and her "sister." Who would be her beloved then, she worried, and who would love her? Having escaped the enslaving existence in the house, she becomes a transformed person. When Paul D. runs into her for the first time after Beloved's disappearance, he is struck by how much stronger and wiser she now appears.

To credit the person Denver has dared become, she is given a line pointing to the essential, summarizing meaning of the "ghostly" title character. Wondering what she finally thinks about Beloved, Paul D. asks her, "You think she sure 'nough your sister?" Denver answers, "At times. At times I think she was—more" (266). What Denver appears to understand is that both roles are possible, in fact, *must* be possible. And in reaching this conclusion and accepting it without flinching, she arrives at an understanding of her full story, past and present—the kind of understanding that all her people need in order to rediscover their love for themselves.

* * * * * * * *

In *Beloved*, Morrison set out to tell a series of stories that would add up to one encompassing story about her people. Holding the stories together so that they would become one was consequently her main aesthetic challenge. She met this challenge by employing two strategies in particular, both of which she has always used, but perhaps never quite so successfully. As in her previous work, she employs a narrative voice based on the idea of a griot's way of spinning a story. This approach works especially well in *Beloved*, not only because of the versatility and spontaneity inherent in this tradition and necessary for this text, but also because of the appropriate fact that the griot is considered a bearer of the culture and history Morrison is trying to pass on. The other unifying strategy Morrison employs with great success is that of natural imagery as a reflective subtext.

Morrison is especially effective in using water and tree imagery. Water imagery abounds because, clearly, Morrison means to make the metaphoric connection between water and life. More specifically, water becomes a metaphor for new life, with the idea of a free life closely associated. Thus, there are allusions to water at those critical points where slave characters cross into freedom and new life in one way or another. More ambiguously, but at the same time appropriately, allusions to water are also made with the birth of Denver and the arrival of Beloved. Water and life, life and death, purposely flow together. This is one way in which the text works, and one of the main lessons about authentic existence.

Morrison's use of tree imagery in *Beloved* is equally expressive, if not more so. The overall intent of the novel, in fact, can be apprehended by tracing this imagery. To begin with, trees can be seen to literally dominate the landscapes of the characters' stories, serving as shelters, companions, comforters, and reminders of the past. These images, in turn, are made to attain the closely related function of unifying the characters and themes into a "whole" story. Not incidentally, trees figure prominently in African religions, signifying the source of life and linking the physical and spiritual worlds.[16] Because this fact lies behind Morrison's use of trees, it becomes clear in the end that the unification she aspires to through this kind of natural imagery is guided more by a religious than an aesthetic vision. Morrison means nothing less than to connect the living with the dead, the physical with the spiritual. This is why in *Beloved* physical, particularly natural, objects often become spiritual in nature. A grove becomes a cathedral, for example, and blackberries transubstantiate into a sacrament. To someone like Paul D., whose racial memory hasn't been severed completely, a tree he calls Brother can provide a mystical relationship that helps him save his spiritual past while living in the physical bonds of the present. Paul D. simply accepts this relationship, never questioning the possibility, because like his ancestors, he accepts the connection between the physical and spiritual worlds as self-evident. Thus he can subsequently accept the possibility that a haunting spirit has moved into Sethe's house. To him, spirits actually exist, and they are a reality that must be dealt with. This is a fact of his African heritage, a fact that should be taken into account in any proper reading of *Beloved*.

By grasping this fact, then, and concentrating on Morrison's use of tree imagery, one can unfold the following overarching story. Although she has never left 124 Bluestone Road since her death—that is, certainly her haunting spirit has never left—Beloved appears after eighteen years, with her new skin and vacant eyes, to claim Sethe. With breath smelling of "bark during the day" and "leaves at night," Beloved is linked to the "tree" of scar tissue on Sethe's back, which she tries to supplant (19). It's not as though Sethe needs to carry an additional burden from her past. Her past consists of such crushing facts as scant knowledge of her own mother, a childhood and adolescence spent in slavery, an obscene rape by two white boys, the loss of her husband, the killing of her daughter, and her repudiation by her two sons. As the years go by, she is left with only her daughter Denver as a living reminder of the past. Of course, the scars on her back are a permanent part of her emotional and cultural baggage; but until Paul D. arrives, she thinks she may manage to forget, or at least hold off the past in a state of sorrowful truce as close to amnesia as possible.

The roots of Sethe's sorrow reach back to Sweet Home, which for her represents a personal hell "hidden in lacy groves" (6). Sethe is ashamed that she remembers the trees better than the Sweet Home men, better even than her own lost children. She admits to herself that "try as she might . . . the sycamores beat out the children every time" (6). For Sethe, trees have supplanted the memories of her lost children because it's less painful to remember trees than to recall her attempted murder of her sons and her desperate slaying of her daughter. Appropriately, she managed the slaying with a saw in her woodshed. That Sethe would rather see her children dead than enslaved doesn't salve her loss. Fearing that Sweet Home will claim Denver, Sethe has remained generally silent about her past, closing her daughter out of a significant part of her life and history.

Paul D.'s reappearance opens doors to the past. His previous eighteen years of rootlessness have barely dimmed the memory of a bit in his mouth. Even more painful are other recollections. He is beset with thoughts about what happened to his brothers and his friend Sixo. He continues to be tormented by the memory of his own imprisonment in Georgia. During all his wandering years prior to his arrival at Sethe's house, he has managed to endure, but not because of any meaningful human connection. Instead, Paul D. has found sustenance throughout his life in trees which to him seem "inviting; things you could trust and be near; talk to" (21). Trees affirm life in the midst of human depravity and literally lead Paul D. to precarious safety when he follows tree blossoms north after his escape from the chain gang in Georgia.

Like Paul D., Denver finds comfort in trees, though hers is a bower of boxwoods, where she is "closed off from the hurt of the hurt world" (28). Here she is visited by the spirit of her sister. Denver's sacred bower is a smaller version of the Clearing, Baby Suggs' sacred grove where her sermons sooth the pain of her listeners. The lesson she preaches is one of loving the flesh, affirming the idea of the unity of flesh and spirit, a cultural idea shredded by white oppression. Sheltered by the Clearing, her people become free to love themselves.

By insisting on the unity of flesh and spirit, Morrison prepares the reader to accept Beloved's double function as a living and dead figure. Then at the end, having made Beloved into a metonymic character, linked to reality through trees and water, Morrison has her fade into the forest, with the surviving community starting to forget her "like a bad dream" (274). This fact seems to insist upon Beloved's utter disappearance. However, the final lines of the novel resist the notion of her loss in a number of ways. The idea of her complete disappearance is countered through several concluding details suggesting the remaining presence of "something"; through the repetition of the ironically loaded idea that this was not a story to "pass on"; and through the suggestive fact that the whole story is framed by her name isolated in the title and the very last line (275). And the idea of Beloved's final loss is also countered through Morrison's concluding references to weather: "By and by all trace is gone, and what is forgotten is not only the footprints but the water too and what is down there. The rest is weather. Not the breath of the disremembered and unaccounted for, but wind in the eaves, or spring ice thawing too quickly. Just weather. Certainly no clamor for a kiss" (275).

Given the force of Morrison's natural metaphors and her increasing penchant for ambiguously pointed language, this ending doesn't suggest a dismissal of Beloved after all. In the final analysis, this ending serves instead as a reminder of the enduring presence of her spirit. For we all feel weather, though we may not take particular notice of it. Always a factor in human life—and significantly also a factor in the perception of human death in African cultures where the wind of weather is taken for the ghostly voice of the ancestors—weather becomes inseparable from the human experience in Morrison's work. Weather finally assumes the greatest thematic possibility. Morrison has always tried to join the abstract and the analytical, the poetic and the historical, the physical and the supernatural, and the spiritual and the real. Prior to *Beloved* she came nearest to entirely succeeding in this connection in *Song of Solomon*. In her other works, the rift between these opposing directions has been sometimes noticeable or even prominent. But in *Beloved*, Morrison has managed to avoid this challenging problem in large part by employing a harmonious kind of imagery, and she has done so by finally inserting the all-embracing idea of weather. This strategy succeeds because the idea of weather as a cosmic unifying reality works perfectly both on the imaginative and the material levels. We don't have to see weather to know of its presence. Thus, we are conclusively led to believe by the force of Morrison's persuasive language that Beloved's spirit has become one with the living air which we call weather. And we are led in turn to believe that during the course of the story Beloved was a kind of living "ghost" that materialized out of the air and took on a flesh and blood existence for Morrison's expressed purpose, which was "making history possible, making memory real."[17]

In all of her novels, Morrison locates a specific place where the passing of seasons, extremes in weather, growth of trees and plants impinge upon the lives of her characters. These organic conditions play literal roles since Morrison employs nature as a fact in her novels. But she also takes nature beyond its immediate contact by transmuting examples of material fact into themes through her natural metaphors. These inclinations represent perhaps her greatest strengths. And because these inclinations leading toward a vision of organic unity never falter in *Beloved*, Morrison has written her most impressive novel thus far.

* * * * * * * *

Morrison's most recent novel, *Jazz*, isn't advertised as such, but it is meant to follow *Beloved* as the second volume of a projected trilogy.[18] This fact may surprise those readers who aren't current with Morrison's ambitions, because *Jazz* doesn't extend the story told in *Beloved* in a conventional way. The characters are new, and so is the location. Even the narrative approach is different. However, in terms of chronology, *Jazz* does pick up roughly where *Beloved* left off and continues the greater story Morrison wishes to tell in her trilogy in progress, the story of her people passing through their American experience, from the days of slavery up to the present.

Jazz centers around Joe and Violet Trace as they struggle to come to terms with their actions and with each other. At 53, Joe has fallen for 18 year old Dorcas and has shot her in a paradoxical attempt to keep her. Violet's response to news of her husband's affair is a fragmenting anger that propels her toward Dorcas' funeral armed with a knife to cut the dead girl's face. Forcibly ejected from the funeral before she can do more than nick the girl, Violet rushes home to release all of her pet birds into the cold winter air, including the parrot who can say "I love you." It takes a long time, in effect the length of the book, before love returns to Joe and Violet's place.

Jazz beings and ends in Harlem of the mid 1920's, but in between the story moves freely in place and time. Winding generally backwards and sideways before coming forward again, the story presents the major characters not only as individuals with private lives but also as representative victims of enormously cruel and powerful racial forces. All the individually named characters have their own stories to tell, and all of these stories are thrown into relief by a backdrop of a nation obsessed with skin color. During the half century that *Jazz* covers, there is apparent progress for black Americans, since they are shown to move from the wretchedness of plantation slavery to self-sufficiency in the city, from complete dispossession to military participation in World War I, from examples of suicidal surrender to examples of cultural self-esteem, from lives driven by silent fear to dancing driven by loud jazz. While there is apparent progress during these years, black Americans are shown continuing to suffer through every kind of cruelty imaginable, from the subtlest insults by whites who think of them as untouchables to outright burning of living, screaming black flesh. This shameful history affects all the characters in *Jazz* even while they are shown to be preoccupied with their own personal problems and obsessions.

Violet, thwarted in her jealous rage for revenge, becomes obsessed with the siren who stole her husband's heart. She begins to visit Dorcas' aunt in order to find out all she can about the girl. The more she finds out about the lives of Dorcas and her aunt, the more her inner healing progresses. When Dorcas' best friend, Felice, eventually begins to visit, Violet arrives at the point where she can again reach for love. What has brought her to this final healing is the fact that she has undergone altering perspectives of all the passionate and pain-filled lives found in Harlem, from the orphaned life of Dorcas to her own.

Because Joe is more contemplative and inward than his wife, his healing takes a different, less erratic route. As he stalks Dorcas, he moves back in time, recalling his hunting skills taught long ago by a surrogate father in Virginia. And as he closes in on his betraying lover, he also recalls his abandonment as a baby and his desperate search for the wild woman said to be his mother. While on his outward journey of death, his inward journey takes him past his many stages of transformation brought on by the necessity of surviving in a world hostile to his color. In the process of reviewing his personal life, he reveals himself in a greater, cultural context. He comes out in the end scarred by history but wholly capable of caring for others again because, like his wife, he will have learned (or relearned) to wholly surrender to the mystery of passionate feelings.

Morrison has written about human passion all her life, but never more systematically than in *Jazz*. She begins by choosing the title because the word originally was a slang term for sexual passion, and of course because the same word attached itself to the most famous kind of black American music, a special kind of music that aspires to come from and produce pure emotion. Appropriately, the text itself then begins with a sound rather than a word as such. "Sth," begins the narrator, and from then on the story flows like an extended piece of progressive, improvised jazz. Like many jazz pieces, the novel has a fast opening, establishing a dominant note and theme, and then it breaks into different parts—various stories (passages) and voices (instruments); various motifs, images, and relative themes. As the novel-jazz piece goes on, it comes back again and again to the dominant issue of human passion. The energizing, life-giving force of jazz originates from mystery, continues with surprises, and ends in a sense of renewal; and this is how the novel works, too. *Jazz* is inspired by the whole range of human feelings. As the complicated story moves along, it modulates back and forth in sometimes very unexpected ways. In the end, human passion is urged on as a creative force, with the narrator telling us that we (the readers, the listeners, and by implication also the participants in the whole story) are "free" to "remake."

A look at the framing structure of *Jazz* shows that it follows its own advice about being free to re-make. It starts with one human triangle (Violet, Joe, and Dorcas) and ends with another (Violet, Joe, and Felice). The first triangle ends with death. As the second triangle forms, it appears it might be destined for the same kind of fate. But instead we are surprised, along with the self conscious narrator, by a new variation. Jazz-like, the two triangles are in counterpoint to each other. They play off against each other with the same kind of echoing harmony found throughout the story, and leave the way free for more echoing variations to come.

Strictly speaking, Violet and Joe are the protagonists of *Jazz*. But the dominant presence is actually the nameless narrator. We are always conscious of this narrator, even while various characters tell their own stories, as we would be of a gifted lead player in a jazz group. Gifted this narrator certainly is, playing language with great precision and understanding. Still, we may not be completely satisfied with the performance. Jazz can be hot, it can be cool. This narrator plays it cool. Perhaps too cool. The novel starts off with news of illicit love, murder, and revenge. It seems we are promised hot, low-down, erotic action. But what follows is described in an unusually dispassionate, lyrically distanced way. One early reviewer of *Jazz*, groping for a proper critical response, finally sounding rather inconclusive, summarized his thoughts about the novel in the following way: "Jazz. You have to feel it."[19] Evidently, this reviewer, though in a less forthright manner, was concluding the same thing as another early reviewer who thought that what was missing in *Jazz* was "the emotional nexus, the moment shorn of all artifice that brings us headlong into the deepest recesses of feeling."[20]

Morrison's nameless narrator is provisional in another way besides emotionally. The question finally arises: where is the narrative voice located? In a real character? The author? The living pages? Morrison's apparent answer is that the narrator is to be found in all three, plus in the imaginative mind of the reader. Her narrative strategy is actually a radical extension of her characteristic call on griots and participatory readers. It is a strategy that invites us to think of the fictional narrator, the author, and the book in our hands as so closely connected that when we hold a copy of *Jazz* we are actually *holding* the narrator, author, and story as living presences that touch us directly enough to make us become part of the story and, if we choose, one of the story tellers. The best way to read the "I" in *Jazz*, then, is both as someone telling about other people and as something in creative process. Such a reading can offer the fullest possible expression to the story, both physical and metaphysical. How well does this strategy work in practice? At this point, the answer has to be: it depends on the reader. The ultimate answer— that is to say, the critically informed answer—will have to wait until we can place *Jazz* in the context of the complete trilogy.

In fact, any possible criticism of *Jazz* has to be tentative because the novel itself has the tentative quality of a self-consciously written middle volume of a trilogy. *Jazz* doesn't seem to have any other critical flash points beyond those arising from questions about the narrator's identification and the narrator's cool sound. But in any event, it's not yet possible to make the same kinds of final assessments as it was in the case of *Beloved*. *Jazz* is a bridging work, raised on the complete foundation of *Beloved* but still progressing toward—what? When we know, when we can read the whole trilogy, *Jazz* may turn out to be full of critical surprises.

While Morrison was writing *Jazz*, she was also giving a series of lectures at Harvard University on American literature.[21] The general theme of these lectures was that classic American writers betrayed themselves and their nation's literature by

marginalizing black Americans and their experiences. Morrison
invited today's critics to address this impoverishing aspect in
our written heritage. She hoped for future writers who would
create believable black characters participating fully as human
beings and Americans. Only if black Americans are as fully
represented as whites would we finally have a true national
literature.

It is a fitting climax to this book about Toni Morrison's fiction to recall that she has done perhaps more than any other
novelist to foster the authentic, inclusive national literature she
has called for. Her six novels, voiced from the triple perspective
of black American woman, bring much of the American experience out of the marginal shadows and help give American literature as a whole a more complete and finer dimension.[22] Thus,
even before she finishes her ambitious trilogy about the historical odyssey of African-Americans, we may already recognize her
as one of our most important "national" novelists.

Notes

Chapter 1

[1] Jane Bakerman, "The Seams Can't Show: An Interview with Toni Morrison," *Black American Literature Forum* 12 (1978): 56.

[2] Gloria Naylor, "Gloria Naylor and Toni Morrison: A Conversation," *Southern Review* 21 (1985): 576.

[3] Naylor 576.

[4] Bakerman 56.

[5] Jean Strouse, "Toni Morrison's Black Magic," *Newsweek* 30 March 1981: 53-54.

[6] Strouse 54.

[7] Strouse 54.

[8] Laura B. Randolph, "The Magic of Toni Morrison," *Ebony* July 1988: 104.

[9] Elsie B. Washington, "Morrison Now," *Essence* October 1987: 136.

[10] Monice Mitchell, "Toni Morrison Chafes at Being Labeled 'Role Model,'" *Charlotte Observer* 2 Sept. 1990: 6c.

[11] Mitchell 6c.

[12] Bakerman 57.

[13] Thomas LeClair, "'The Language Must Not Sweat,'" *New Republic* 21 March 1981: 27.

[14] LeClair 27.

[15] LeClair 26.

[16] Claudia Tate, ed., *Black Women Writers at Work* (New York: Continuum, 1983) 126.

[17] Anthony J. Berret, "Toni Morrison's Literary Jazz," *C. L. A. Journal* 32 (March 1989): 267.

[18] Judith Wilson, "A Conversation with Toni Morrison," *Essence* July 1981: 133.

[19] Nellie McKay, "An Interview with Toni Morrison," *Contemporary Literature* 24 (1983): 429.

[20] LeClair 27-28.

[21] McKay 421.

[22] McKay 427.

[23] McKay 427.

[24] Toni Morrison, "Memory, Creation, and Writing" *Thought* 59 (December 1984): 121.

[25] LeClair 26.

[26] LeClair 28.

[27] McKay 424.

[28] Tate 126-27.

[29] LeClair 28.

[30] Tate 120-121.

[31] Tate 121.

[32] McKay 420.

[33] Vashti Crutcher Lewis, "African Tradition in Toni Morrison's *Sula*," *Wild Women in the Whirlwind*, ed. by Joanne M. Braxton and Andre Nicola McLaughlin (New Brunswick, N. J.: Rutgers University Press, 1990) 323.

[34] Terry Otten, *The Crime of Innocence in the Fiction of Toni Morrison* (Columbia: University of Missouri Press, 1989) 82.

[35] Wilfred D. Samuels and Clenora Hudson-Weems, *Toni Morrison* (Boston: Twayne Publishers, 1990) 139.

Chapter 2

[1] Jane Bakerman, "The Seams Can't Show: An Interview with Toni Morrison," *Black American Literature Forum* 12 (1978): 60.

[2] Toni Morrison, "The Site of Memory," *Inventing the Truth: The Art and Craft of Memoir*, ed. by William Zinsser (Boston: Houghton Mifflin, 1987) 110.

[3] Bakerman 60.

[4] Sandi Russell, "It's O. K. to Say O. K.," *Critical Essays on Toni Morrison* ed. by Nellie McKay (Boston: G. K. Hall, 1988) 44.

[5] Richard O. Moore, dir., "The Writer in America," Perspective Films, 1978.

[6] This is not to devalue pursuing a single theme in a critical study. For fine discussions see the following: Terry Otten, *The Crime of Innocence in the Fiction of Toni Morrison* (Columbia: University of Missouri Press, 1989); Jane S. Bakerman, "Failures of Love: Female Initiation in the Novels of Toni Morrison," *American Literature* 52 (1981): 541-63; and Barbara Christian, "Community and Nature: The Novels of Toni Morrison," *Journal of Ethnic Studies* 7 (1980): 65-78.

[7] Claudia Tate, "Toni Morrison," *Black Women Writers at Work*, ed. by Claudia Tate (New York: Continuum, 1983) 125.

[8] Chiwenye Ogunyemi, "Order and Disorder in Toni Morrison's *The Bluest Eye*," *Critique* 19 (1977): 112.

[9] For a further discussion, see Anthony J. Berret, "Toni Morrison's Literary Jazz," *C. L. A. Journal* 32 (1989): 267-283.

[10] Toni Morrison, *The Bluest Eye* (New York: Washington Square Press, 1970) 9. Subsequent references will be noted in parentheses.

[11] For a full discussion, see Barbara Christian, "Community and Nature: The Novels of Toni Morrison," *Journal of Ethnic Studies* 7 (1980): 65-78.

[12] Barbara Christian, "Community and Nature": 66; and Susan Willis, "Eruptions of Funk: Historicizing Toni Morrison," *Black American Literature Forum* 16 (1982): 35.

[13] See also Robert Sargent, "A Way of Ordering Experience," *Faith of a (Woman) Writer*, ed. by Alice Kessler-Harris and William McBrien (Westport: Greenwood Press, 1988) 229-36; and Elizabeth B. House, "Artists and the Art of Living: Order and Disorder in Toni Morrison's Fiction," *Modern Fiction Studies* 34 (1988): 27-44.

[14] Ogunyemi 118.

[15] Ogunyemi 112.

[16] Ogunyemi 112.

[17] See also Phyllis Klotman, "Dick and Jane and the Shirley Temple Sensibility in *The Bluest Eye,*" *Black American Literature Forum* 13 (1979): 123-25.

Chapter 3

[1] Claudia Tate, "Toni Morrison," *Black Women Writers at Work*, ed. by Claudia Tate (New York: Continuum, 1983) 128.

[2] Toni Morrison, "Memory, Creation, and Writing" *Thought* 59 (December 1984): 389.

[3] Deborah E. McDowell, "'The Self and the Other': Reading Toni Morrison's *Sula* and the Black Female Text," *Critical Essays on Toni Morrison*, ed. by Nellie Y. McKay (Boston: G. K. Hall, 1988) 80.

[4] Robert B. Stepto, "'Intimate Things in Place': A Conversation with Toni Morrison," *Massachusetts Review* 18 (1977): 474.

[5] Toni Morrison, *Sula* (New York: Alfred A. Knopf, 1974) 4. Subsequent references will be noted in parentheses.

[6] Barbara Christian, "'Community and Nature: The Novels of Toni Morrison," *Journal of Ethnic Studies* 7 (1980): 53.

[7] McDowell 82.

[8] McDowell 82.

[9] Stepto 476.

[10] Stepto 487.

[11] Valerie Smith, *Self-Discovery and Authority in Afro-American Narrative* (Cambridge, Massachusetts: Harvard University Press, 1987) 135.

[12] Terry Otten, *The Crime of Innocence in the Fiction of Toni Morrison* (Columbia: University of Missouri Press, 1989) 42.

[13] Meditation XVII, *Devotions*.

[14] Richard O. Moore, dir., "The Writer in America," Perspective Films, 1978.

[15] Stepto 477.

[16] Stepto 476.

Chapter 4

[1] Cynthia Davis, "Self, Society, and Myth in Toni Morrison's Fiction," *Contemporary Literature* 23 (1982): 336.

[2] James H. Evans, "The Recovery of Sacred Myth: Toni Morrison's *Song of Solomon*," *Spiritual Enpowerment in Afro-American Literature* (Lewiston, New York: Edwin Mellen Press, 1987) 159.

[3] Evans 160.

[4] Toni Morrison, *Song of Solomon* (New York: Alfred A. Knopf, 1977) 18. Subsequent references will be noted in parentheses.

[5] See: John Mbiti, *African Religion and Philosophy* (New York: Garden City, 1970).

[6] Philip M. Royster, "Milkman's Flying; The Scapegoat Transcended in Toni Morrison's *Song of Solomon*," *C. L. A. Journal* 24 (June 1982): 433.

[7] Grace Ann Hovet and Barbara Lounsberry, "Flying as Symbol and Legend in Toni Morrison's *The Bluest Eye, Sula,* and *Song of Solomon*," *C. L. A. Journal* 27 (1983): 120.

[8] Genevieve Fabré, "Genealogical Archeology or the Quest for Legacy in Toni Morrison's *Song of Solomon*," *Critical Essays on Toni Morrison*, ed. by Nellie Y. McKay (Boston: G. K. Hall, 1988) 110.

[9] Nellie McKay, "An interview with Toni Morrison," *Contemporary Literature* 24 (1983): 417.

[10] Robert B. Stepto, "'Intimate Things in Place': A Conversation with Toni Morrison," *Massachusetts Review* 18(1977): 487.

[11] McKay 415.

[12] Valerie Smith, *Self-Discovery and Authority in Afro-American Literature* (Cambridge, Massachusetts: Harvard University Press, 1987) 144.

[13] Barbara Christian, "Community and Nature: The Novels of Toni Morrison," *Journal of Ethnic Studies* 7 (Winter 1980): 73.

[14] Smith 152.

[15] Stepto 482.

[16] Melvin Dixon, *Ride Out the Wilderness* (Urbana: University of Illinois Press, 1987) 158.

[17] Claudia Tate, "Toni Morrison," *Black Women Writers* (New York: Continuum, 1983) 125.

[18] Barbara Christian, *Black Feminist Criticism: Perspectives on Black Women Writers* (New York: Pergamon Press, 1985) 61.

[19] Terry Otten, *The Crime of Innocence in the Fiction of Toni Morrison* (Columbia: University of Missouri Press, 1989) 57.

[20] See: Gerry Brenner, "*Song of Solomon*: Rejecting Rank's Monomyth and Feminism," *Critical Essays on Toni Morrison*, ed. by Nellie Y. McKay (Boston: G. K. Hall, 1988) 123; and Davis 341.

[21] McKay 419.

[22] Jane S. Bakerman, "'Failures in Love: Female Initiation in the Novels of Toni Morrison," *American Literature* 52 (January 1981): 563.

Chapter 5

[1] Nellie McKay, "An Interview with Toni Morrison," *Contemporary Literature* 24 (1983): 416-17.

[2] Pearl K. Bell, "Self-Seekers," *Commentary* August 1981: 57.

[3] Jean Strouse, "Toni Morrison's Black Magic," *Newsweek* 30 March 1981: 57.

[4] See Pearl K. Bell, for example: Bell 57.

[5] Morrison is particularly explicit on this subject in her essay that appeared in *Thought*: Toni Morrison, "Memory, Creation, and Writing," *Thought* 59 December 1984: 389-90.

[6] Toni Morrison, *Tar Baby* (New York: Alfred A. Knopf, 1981) 53. Subsequent references will be noted in parentheses.

[7] See especially Terry Otten's full-length study of this theme: Terry Otten, *The Crime of Innocence in the Fiction of Toni Morrison* (Columbia: University of Missouri Press, 1989).

[8] McKay 422.

[9] McKay 422.

[10] Wilfred D. Samuels and Clenora Hudson-Weems, *Toni Morrison* (Boston: Twayne Publishers, 1990) 91.

[11] Judith Wilson, "A Conversation with Toni Morrison," *Essence* July 1981: 86.

[12] Wilson 86.

[13] Wilson 86.

[14] Barbara Christian, *Black Feminist Criticism: Perspectives on Black Women Writers* (New York: Pergamon Press, 1985) 67.

[15] Bell 57.

[16] James Coleman, "The Quest for Wholeness in Toni Morrison's *Tar Baby*," *Black American Literature Forum* 20 (1986): 72.

[17] Evelyn Hawthorne, "On Gaining the Double-Vision: *Tar Baby* as Diasporean Novel," *Black American Literature Forum* 22 (1988): 105.

[18] McKay 424-25.

[19] Wilson 133.

Chapter 6

[1] Bonnie Angelo, "Interview: The Pain of Being Black," *Time* 22 May 1989: 120.

[2] Gloria Naylor, "A Conversation: Gloria Naylor and Toni Morrison," *Southern Review* 21 (1985): 583.

[3] Naylor 584.

[4] Walter Clemons, "A Gravestone of Memories," *Time* 28 Sept. 1987: 74-75.

[5] Angelo 120.

[6] Marsha Darling, "In the Realm of Responsibility: A Conversation with Toni Morrison," *Women's Review of Books* V March 1988: 5.

[7] Clemons 75.

[8] Naylor 585.

[9] Darling 5.

[10] This "fleshly" and consequently incomplete reading of *Beloved* has continued right up to the present. Thus, for example, Barbara Schapiro in her 1991 article presents an ingenious reading of the novel that in the final analysis isn't entirely satisfactory because it unavoidably leaves out the Middle Passage factor. See: Barbara Schapiro, "The Bonds of Love and Boundaries of Self in Toni Morrison's *Beloved*," *Contemporary Literature* 32 Summer 1991: 194-210.

[11] Wilfred D. Samuels and Clenora Hudson-Weems, *Toni Morrison* (Boston: Twayne Publishers, 1990) 94.

[12] Darling 5.

[13] Darling 5.

[14] Vashti Crutcher Lewis, "African Tradition in Toni Morrison's *Sula*," *Wild Women in the Whirlwind: Afra-American Culture and the Contemporary Literary Renaissance* edited by Joanne M. Braxton and Andree Nicola McLaughlin (New Brunswick, N. J.: Rutgers University Press, 1990) 318.

[15] Toni Morrison, *Beloved* (New York: Alfred A. Knopf, 1987) 51. Subsequent references will be noted in parentheses.

[16] John Mbiti, *African Religions and Philosophy* (New York: Garden City, 1970) 66.

[17] Darling 6.

[18] Toni Morrison, *Jazz* (New York: Alfred A. Knopf, 1992).

[19] Christopher Lehmann-Haupt, "Books of The Times" *New York Times* 2 April 1992: 30.

[20] Edna O'Brien, "The Clearest Eye: *Jazz*" *New York Times Book Review* 5 April 1992: 30.

[21] The lectures were collected and published by Harvard University Press: *Playing in the Dark: Whiteness and the Literary Imagination* (Cambridge, Mass.: Harvard University Press, 1992).

[22] Wendy Steiner, "The Clearest Eye: *Playing in the Dark*" *New York Times Book Review* 5 April 1992: 17.

Bibliography

Novels of Toni Morrison

The Bluest Eye. New York: Holt, Rinehart, & Winston, 1970.
Sula. New York: Alfred A. Knopf, 1973.
Song of Solomon. New York: Alfred A. Knopf, 1977.
Tar Baby. New York: Alfred A. Knopf, 1981.
Beloved. New York: Alfred A. Knopf, 1987.
Jazz. New York: Alfred A. Knopf, 1992.

Nonfiction by Toni Morrison

"Rediscovering Black History." *New York Times Magazine* 11 August 1974: 14, 16, 18, 20, 22, 24.
The Black Book. Ed. by Toni Morrison and compiled by Middleton Harris. New York: Random House, 1974.
"Behind the Making of *The Black Book.*" *Black World* 23 (1974): 86-90.
"Reading." *Mademoiselle* May 1975: 14.
"A Slow Walk of a Tree (as Grandmother Would Say), Hopeless (as Grandfather Would Say)." *New York Times Magazine* 4 July 1976: 104, 150, 152, 160, 162, 164.
"I Will Always Be A Writer." *Essence* December 1976: 54-56, 90.
"Memory, Creation, and Writing." *Thought* 59 (December, 1984): 385-90.
"A Knowing So Deep." *Essence* May 1985: 230.
"The Site of Memory." *Inventing the Truth: The Art and Craft of Memoir.* Ed. by William Zinsser. Boston: Houghton Mifflin, 1987, 103-24.
Playing in the Dark: Whiteness and the Literary Imagination. Cambridge, Mass.: Harvard University Press, 1992.

Interviews

Angelo, Bonnie. "The Pain of Being Black." *Time* 133 (22 May, 1989): 120-23.

Bakerman, Jane. "The Seams Can't Show: An Interview with Toni Morrison." *Black American Literature Forum* 12 (1978): 56-60.

Darling, Marsha. "In the Realm of Responsibility." *Women's Review of Books* 5 (March, 1988): 5-6.

Davis, Christina. "Interview with Toni Morrison." *Presence Africaine* 145 (1988): 141-50.

Harper, Michael, and Robert Stepto, eds. "Interview." *Chant of Saints*. Urbana: University of Illinois Press, 1979. 213-29.

Horn, Miriam. "Five Years of Terror." *US News and World Report*. 19 October 1987: 75.

Koenen, Anne. "The One Out of Sequence: An Interview with Toni Morrison, New York, April 1980." *History and Tradition in Afro-American Culture*. Ed. by Gunter H. Lenz. Frankfurt, Germany: Campus, 1984. 207-21.

LeClair, Thomas. "The Language Must Not Sweat." *New Republic* 21 March 1981: 25-29.

Lester, Rosemarie K. "An Interview with Toni Morrison, Hessian Radio Network, Frankfurt, West Germany." *Critical Essays on Toni Morrison*. Ed. by Nellie Y. McKay. Boston: G. K. Hall, 1988. 47-54.

McKay, Nellie. "An Interview with Toni Morrison." *Contemporary Literature* 24 (Winter, 1983): 413-29.

Mitchell, Monice. "Toni Morrison Chafes At Being Labeled 'Role Model.'" *Charlotte Observer* 2 September, 1990: 6c.

Naylor, Gloria. "Gloria Naylor and Toni Morrison: A Conversation." *Southern Review* 21 (1985): 567-93.

Parker, Bettye J. "Complexity: Toni Morrison's Women: An Interview Essay." *Sturdy Black Bridges: Visions of Black Women in Literature*. Ed. by Roseann P. Bell, Bettye J. Parker and Beverly Guy-Sheftall. Garden City, New York: Doubleday (Anchor), 1979. 251-257.

"Person to Person." *Black Seeds* (London) 1 (1980): 28-29.

Shange, Ntozake. "Interview with Toni Morrison." *American Rag* November 1978: 48-52.

Stepto, Robert B. "'Intimate Things in Place': A Conversation with Toni Morrison." *Massachusetts Review* 18 (1977): 473-89.

Tate, Claudia. "Toni Morrison." *Black Women Writers at Work*. New York: Continuum, 1983. 117-31.

Washington, Elsie B. "Toni Morrison Now." *Essence* October 1987: 58, 136-37.

Watkins, Mel. "Talk with Toni Morrison." *New York Times Book Review* 11 September 1977: 48, 50.

Wilson, Judith. "Conversation with Toni Morrison." *Essence* 12 (July, 1981): 84, 86, 128, 130, 133-34.

Books on Toni Morrison

Harris, Trudier. *Fiction and Folklore: The Novels of Toni Morrison*. Knoxville, Tennessee: University of Tennessee Press, 1991. Places Morrison in the extensive line of black writers who have drawn for their subject matter on the folk traditions passed on by African-Americans through the gen-

erations. Shows at the same time how Morrison transforms this tradition through her art, and stresses especially how she uses reversal of
folklore as a deliberate strategy.

Holloway, Karla F. C., and Stephanie Demetrakopoulous. *New Directions of
Spirituality: A Biracial, Bicultural Reading of the Novels of Toni Morrison.* Greenwood, Connecticut: Greenwood Press, 1987. Coming from
different racial and cultural backgrounds, the authors attempt to add a
new understanding of Morrison's work by means of placing their findings
about the primary values of the texts and their symbolic realities
against each other.

Jones, Bessie W., and Audrey I. Vinson. *The World of Toni Morrison: Exploration in Literary Criticism.* Dubuque, Iowa: Kendall-Hunt, 1985. Provides a view of various workable approaches to the fiction of Morrison
preceding *Beloved.*

McKay, Nellie Y., ed. *Critical Essays on Toni Morrison.* Boston: G. K. Hall,
1988. Contains reviews of the first four novels, two interviews, and several analytical articles focusing on individual novels and ranging over
Morrison's work as a whole. Most of these articles were written specifically for this collection.

Otten, Terry. *The Crime of Innocence in the Fiction of Toni Morrison.* Columbia:
University of Missouri Press, 1989. Argues that Morrison's work, while
featuring the black experience in America, has a universal mythic perspective in the end, particularly in that all her novels focus on the idea
of the "fortunate fall."

Samuels, Wilfred D., and Clenora Hudson-Weems. *Toni Morrison.* Boston:
Twayne Publishers, 1990. Focuses on the issue of self-discovery in an existential context, along with taking a look at Morrison's style and other
special thematic features, such as her exploration of life in the black
community.

Articles on Toni Morrison

Atlas, Marilyn Judith. "The Darker Side of Toni Morrison's *Song of Solomon.*"
Society for the Study of Midwestern Literature Newsletter 10 (1980): 1-
13. Looks at the deeply troublesome underside concerns of *Song of
Solomon.*

—. "A Woman Both Shiny and Brown: Feminine Strength in Toni Morrison's
Song of Solomon." *Society for the Study of Midwestern Literature
Newsletter* 9 (1979): 8-12. Focuses on the main attributes of women
characters in *Song of Solomon.*

Bakerman, Jane S. "Failures of Love: Female Initiation in the Novels of Toni
Morrison." *American Literature* 52 (January. 1981): 541-63. Discusses
the search for self-identity which the main characters undergo in the
first three novels. Places emphasis on the apparent failed initiations
into life some of the characters experience.

Banyiwa-Horne, Naama. "The Scary Face of the Self: An Analysis of the

Character of Sula." *Sage* 2 (1985): 28-31. Discusses Sula and the idea of her alter ego in the context of her darker aspects.

Barksdale, Richard K. "Castration Symbolism in Recent Black American Fiction." *C. L. A. Journal* 29 (1986): 400-413. Examines black male characters and the issue of castration in several novels by black women writers, including Morrison's *Sula*.

Bell, Pearl K. "Self Seekers." *Commentary* 72 (August, 1981): 56-60. Analyzes the main characters' search for identity in *Tar Baby* in the process of discussing other books dealing with this same theme.

Berret, Anthony J. "Toni Morrison's Literary Jazz." *C. L. A. Journal* 32 (March, 1989): 267-83. Observes "eye" motif and contrasts it with jazz in the first four novels. Provides a general exploration of jazz music principles used in these books.

Bischoff, Joan. "The Novels of Toni Morrison: Studies in Thwarted Sensibility." *Studies in Black Literature* 6 (1975): 21-23. Investigates the problems of the female protagonists in the first two novels, especially their being overly sensitive to thrive in their harsh world.

Blake, Susan I. "Folklore and Community in *Song of Solomon*." *Melus* 7 (1980): 71-82. Concerned with the use of myth as a means toward the goal of wholeness.

—. "Toni Morrison." *Afro-American Fiction Writers After 1955: Dictionary of Literary Biography*. Ed. by Thadious M. Davis and Trudier Harris. Detroit: Gale Research Co., 1984. 187-99. Provides a biographical note and a summary of Morrison's work.

Bogus, S. D. "An Authored Tie-up: The Wedding of Symbol and Point of View in Toni Morrison's *Sula*." *C. L. A. Journal* 33 (1989): 73-80. Looks at how symbols and the use of narrative perspective are connected in *Sula*.

Bowman, Diane Kim. "Flying High: The American Icarus in Morrison, Roth, and Updike." *Perspectives on Contemporary Literature* 8 (1982): 10-17. Discusses Morrison's use of the Icarus myth along with how Roth and Updike also use it.

Brenner, Gerry. "*Song of Solomon*: Morrison's Rejection of Rank's Monomyth and Feminism." *Studies in American Fiction* 15 (Spring, 1987): 13-24. Considers Morrison's use of the monomyth as a basis in *Song of Solomon*, with a special emphasis placed on the presentation of Pilate.

Bruck, Peter. "Returning to One's Roots." *The Afro-American Novel Since 1960*. Ed. by Peter Bruck and Wolfgang Karrer. Amsterdam: Gruner, 1982. 289-305. Places focus on folklore, especially on the motifs of searching and flying, while discussing the issue of self-affirmation of the major characters.

Blusterbaum, Allison A. "'Sugarman Gone Home': Folksong in Toni Morrison's *Song of Solomon*." *Publications of the Arkansas Philological Association* 10 (Spring, 1984): 15-28. Addresses the issue of how folklore, especially song, functions in *Song of Solomon*.

Butler, Robert James. "Open Movement and Selfhood in Toni Morrison's *Song of*

Solomon." *Centennial Review* 28-29 (Fall-Winter, 1984-85): 58-75. Looks at the direction toward self-discovery found in *Song of Solomon.*

Butler-Evans, Elliott. *Race, Gender, and Desire: Narrative Strategies in the Fiction on Toni Cade Bambara, Toni Morrison, and Alice Walker.* Philadelphia: Temple University Press, 1989. Analyzes Morrison's fictional technique along with those of two other prominent black women writers.

Byerman, Keith. "Intense Behaviors: The Use of the Grotesque in *The Bluest Eye* and *Eva's Man.*" *C. L. A. Journal* 25 (1982): 447-57. Provides a comparative analysis of *The Bluest Eye* and *Eva's Man,* focusing on their use of the conventions of the grotesque.

Campbell, Josie P. "To Sing the Song, To Tell the Tale." *Comparative Literature Studies* 20 (1985): 394-412. Offers a comparative study of Morrison's *Song of Solomon* and *Tar Baby* and two novels by the Guadeloupe writers, with an emphasis placed on the theme of the search for self.

Capland, Brina. "A Fierce Conflict of Colors." *Nation* 2 My 1981: 529, 530, 534-35. Shows how much of the argument taking place in *Tar Baby* is expressed through a symbolic use of colors.

Christian, Barbara. "Community and Nature: The Novels of Toni Morrison." *Journal of Ethnic Studies* 7 (Winter, 1980): 65-78. Studies the link between Morrison's characters' "belief system" and their conception of nature. Concludes that this connecting theme is one of the main reasons why Morrison's writing gives off a sense of "timelessness" while at the same time grounded in "the specificity" of her characters and their communities.

—. "Community and Nature: The Novels of Toni Morrison (1980)." *Black Feminist Criticism: Perspectives on Black Women Writers.* New York: Pergamon Press, 1985. 47-63. Same content as in above item.

—. "The Concept of Class in the Novels of Toni Morrison (1981)." *Black Feminist Criticism: Perspectives on Black Women Writers.* New York: Pergamon Press, 1985. 71-80. Finds that Morrison's concept of class, as she uses it, is deeply rooted in history. Indicates how Morrison tends to create characters who represent specific social values.

—. "The Contemporary Fables of Toni Morrison." *Black Women Novelists.* Westport, Connecticut: Greenwood Press, 1980. 137-79. Analyzes the major female characters and the culture clash of black against white, and looks closely at the relationship between Morrison's use of stylistics and themes.

—. "From the Inside Out: Afro-American Women Literary Tradition and the State." *Center for Humanities Studies Occasional Papers.* University of Minnesota Press, 1986. Provides a general discussion of black women writers and the question of their history as passed on by their mothers.

—. "Pass It On." *Black Women Novelists.* Westport, Connecticut: Greenwood Press, 1980. 239-52. Gives an overview of Morrison's female characters in the earlier fiction.

—. "Testing the Strength of the Black Culture Bond: Review of Toni Morrison's *Tar Baby* (1981)." New York: Pergamon Press, 1985. 65-69. Reprints a review which noted Morrison's use of the tar baby story and found fault with her use of certain stereotypes.

—. "Trajectories of Self-Definition: Placing Contemporary Afro-American Women's Fiction." *Black Feminist Criticism: Perspectives of Black Women Writers.* New York: Pergamon Press, 1985. 171-86. Concentrates on what black women are up against in America when seeking self-definition and personal affirmation.

Clemons, Walter. "A Gravestone of Memories." *Newsweek* 28 September 1987: 74-76. Reviews *Beloved*, touting it as a masterpiece about post-Civil War black life.

Clark, Norris. "Flying Back: Toni Morrison's *The Bluest Eye, Sula*, and *Song of Solomon*." *Minority Voices* 4 (Fall, 1980): 51-63. Traces the thematic idea of flying through the first three novels.

Coleman, James. "The Quest for Wholeness in Morrison's *Tar Baby*." *Black American Literature Forum* 20 (1986): 62-73. Considers the community and the quest for a whole life as found in *Tar Baby*.

Cowart, David. "Faulkner and Joyce in Morrison's *Song of Solomon*." *American Literature* 62 (March, 1990): 87-101. Corresponds the writing found in *Song of Solomon* and the writing of Faulkner and Joyce.

Cummings, Kate. "Claiming the Mother('s) Tongue: *Beloved, Ceremony, Mothers and Shadows*." *College English* 52 (September, 1990): 552-569. Discusses *Beloved* along with two other books, showing that all three are stories of resistance that are written from the perspective of minorities.

Davis, Christina. "*Beloved*: A Question of Identity." *Presence Africaine* 145 (1988): 151-56. Focuses on the issue of self-identification in *Beloved*.

Davis, Cynthia A. "Self, Society, and Myth in Toni Morrison's Fiction." *Contemporary Literature* 23 (Summer, 1982): 323-42. Discusses the conflict of individual vs. community found in the first three novels, with a consideration of how the ideas and values of myths work to define reality, especially in the case of Morrison's female characters.

De Arman, Charles. "Milkman as the Archetypal Hero: 'Thursday's Child Has Far to Go.'" *Obsidian* 6 (Winter, 1980): 56-59. Reveals the mythical strains found in the protagonist of *Song of Solomon*.

De Weever, Jacqueline. "The Inverted World of Toni Morrison's *The Bluest Eye* and *Sula*." *C. L. A. Journal* 22 (1979): 402-414. Examines Morrison's use of inversions, showing in the process how "black" her vision is, since an inverted world does not allow a healthy self-image.

—. "Toni Morrison's Use of Fairy Tales, Folk Tales, and Myth in *Song of Solomon*." *Southern Folklore Quarterly* 44 (1980): 131-44. Describes Morrison's deliberate use of fairy tales, folklore, and mythology as part of her method in *Song of Solomon*.

Dickerson, Vanessa D. "The Naked Father in Toni Morrison's *The Bluest Eye*."

Refiguring the Father. Ed. by Patricia Yaeger. Carbondale: University of Illinois Press, 1989. 108-127. Concentrates on the father figure in Morrison's first novel.

Dittmar, Linda. "'Will the Circle Be Unbroken?' The Politics of Form in *the Bluest Eye.*" *Novel: A Forum on Fiction* 23 (Winter, 1980): 137-47. Looks at the politics and relates them to the form of Morrison's first novel.

Dixon, Melvin. *Ride Out the Wilderness: Geography and Identity in Afro-American Literature.* Urbana: University of Illinois Press, 1987. 141-69. Discusses Morrison's achievement of form and art based on her first three novels. Emphasizes her use of physical and cultural geography.

Domini, John. "Toni Morrison's *Sula*: An Inverted Inferno." *High Plains Literary Review* 3 (Spring, 1988): 75-90. Considers the inversion of the inferno idea found in Morrison's second novel.

Dowling, Colette. "The Song of Toni Morrison." *New York Times Magazine* 20 May 1979: 40-42. Gives a look at Morrison's life and provides plot summaries.

Edelberg, Cynthia Dubin. "Morrison's Voices: Formal Education, the Work Ethic, and the Bible." *American Literature* 58 (May, 1986): 217-37. Makes the case that Morrison's narrative voice suggests the failure of religion, education, and the work ethic as possible means of salvation. Points out that Morrison really concludes that formal education for blacks is destructive.

Editorial. "The Toni Award." *New Republic* 19 June 1989: 9-11. Complains about some of Morrison's publicly stated views.

Erickson, Peter B. "Images of Nurturance in Toni Morrison's *Tar Baby.*" *C. L. A. Journal* 28 (September, 1984): 11-32. Focuses on Morrison's handling of the issue of nurturing in *Tar Baby.*

Evans, James H. "The Recovery of Sacred Myth: Toni Morrison's *Song of Solomon.*" *Spiritual Empowerment in Afro-American Literature.* Lewiston, New York: Edwin Mellen Press, 1987. 131-61. Concentrates on Morrison's use of myth in *Song of Solomon.*

Fick, Thomas H. "Toni Morrison's 'Allegory of the Caves': Movies, Consumption, and Platonic Realism in *The Bluest Eye.*" *Journal of the Midwestern Modern Language Association* 22 (Spring, 1989): 10-22. Gives *The Bluest Eye* an allegorical reading, emphasizing contemporary influences of movies, consumerism, and idealized realism.

Fields, Karen E. "To Embrace Dead Strangers: Toni Morrison's *Beloved.*" *Mother Puzzles: Daughters and Mothers in Contemporary American Literature.* Ed. by Mickey Pearlman. Westport, Connecticut: 1989. 159-69. Provides a look at the treatment of mother-daughter love found in *Beloved.*

Fishman, Charles. "Naming Names: Three Recent Novels by Women Writers." *Names* 32 (March, 1984): 33-44. Discusses Morrison's use of names in *Tar Baby*, one of three novels under comparative consideration.

Freiert, William K. "Classical Themes in Toni Morrison's *Song of Solomon*." *Helios* 10 (1983): 161-70. Discusses Morrison's use of classical myths, notably five Western myths, in *Song of Solomon*.

Gibson, Donald B. "Text and Countertext in Toni Morrison's *The Bluest Eye*." *LIT* 1 (December, 1989): 19-32. Sets the outer text against a countertext running through Morrison's first novel.

Gillespie, Marcia Ann. "Toni Morrison." *Ms Magazine* January 1988: 60-62. Focuses on Morrison's women characters and the essential questions and problems they face.

Hadas, Rachel. "Four Writers." *Partisan Review* Spring 1989: 310-17. Includes a comparative look at *Beloved* in this essay reviewing four related publications.

Harris, A. Leslie. "Myths as Structure in Toni Morrison's *Song of Solomon*." *Melus* 7 (1980): 69-76. Considers Morrison's use of myths in *Song of Solomon*, especially how they function in shaping the text.

Harris, Trudier. "Denial of the Ritual." *Exorcising Blackness: Historical and Literary Lynching and Burning Rituals*. Bloomington, Indiana: Indiana University Press, 1984. 149-62. Shows how Morrison is concerned with the mythical aspects of history, focusing on the myth of the white fear of blacks' rapist fantasies of white women.

Hawthorne, Evelyn. "On Gaining the Double Vision: *Tar Baby* as Diasporean Novel." *Black American Literature Forum* 22 (1988): 97-107. Takes up the issue of diaspora, particularly with reference to Son. Argues that the novel's ending underlines the conclusion that Son's future is promising, and that in fact *Tar Baby* has an optimistic ending.

House, Elizabeth B. "Artists and the Art of Living: Order and Disorder in Toni Morrison's Fiction." *Modern Fiction Studies* 34 (Spring, 1988): 27-44. Shows that one of Morrison's central themes is the importance of balancing lives between order and disorder, with a creative activity being the main means of providing this necessary balance.

—. "The 'Sweet Life' in Toni Morrison's Fiction." *American Literature* 56 (May, 1984): 181-202. Shows how Morrison juxtaposes characters as they are guided by the two modes of living, the idyllic and the success-oriented.

Hovet, Grace Ann. "Principles of Perception in Toni Morrison's *Sula*." *Black American Literature Forum* 13 (1979): 126-29. Reveals how in *Sula* Morrison deals with the importance of saving one's identity in an unstable world.

Hovet, Grace Ann, and Barbara Lounsberry. "Flying as Symbol and Legend in Toni Morrison's *The Bluest Eye, Sula,* and *Song of Solomon*." *C. L. A. Journal* 27 (1983): 119-40. Discusses Morrison's use of flying and flight imagery in her first three novels. Argues that she extends this kind of imagery, common in Afro-American literature, in significant ways.

Howard, Maureen. "A Novel of Exile and Home." *New Republic* 21 March 1981: 29-30, 32. Reviews *Tar Baby*, focusing on the major characters and their individual histories.

Howitz, D. "Nameless Ghosts: Possession and Dispossession in *Beloved*." *Studies in American Fiction* 17 (August, 1989): 157-67. Analyzes Morrison's use of "ghosts" in *Beloved*, noting how they function in relation to thematic concerns.

Hudson-Withers, Clenora. "The World of Topsy-Turvydom in Toni Morrison's Fiction." *Western Journal of Black Studies* 10 (1986): 132-36. Describes the problem of existence in an upside-down world (i. e. Western) that Morrison's characters face. Shows that the characters respond to such a world by inverse behavior.

Iannone, Carol. "Toni Morrison's Career." *Commentary* 84 (1987): 59-63. Takes a look at Morrison's life and provides an overview of her career.

Joyce, Joyce Ann. "Structural and Thematic Unity in Toni Morrison's *Song of Solomon*." *CEA Critic* 49 (Winter-Summer, 1986-87): 185-98. Shows the designed connection between theme and structure in *Song of Solomon*.

Klotman, Phyllis R. "Dick-and-Jane and the Shirley Temple Sensibility in *The Bluest Eye*." *Black American Literature Forum* 13 (1979): 123-25. Discusses "Dick and Jane" and Shirley Temple as ironic contrasts for a black child's educational experience.

Lange, Bonnie Shipman. "Toni Morrison's Rainbow Code." *Critique* 24 (1983): 173-81. Studies Morrison's use of color imagery and argues that each key color is used by her to inspire certain representative reactions.

Lee, Dorothy H. "The Quest for Self: Triumph and Failure in the Works of Toni Morrison." *Black Women Writers* (1950-1980). Ed. by Mari Evans. New York: Doubleday, 1984. 346-66. Investigates the use of the self-discovery theme found in Morrison's earlier works.

—. "*Song of Solomon*: To Ride the Air." *Black American Literature Forum* 16 (Summer, 1982): 64-70. Looks at *Song of Solomon* as a pilgrimage story that is based on aspects of the monomyth.

Lee, Valerie Gray. "The Use of Folktale in Novels by Black Women Writers." *C. L. A. Journal* 23 (1980): 266-72. Discusses Morrison's use of folktales in *Sula*, in connection with the work of two other women novelists. Argues that the return to the use of metaphorical folktales is an increasing trend in modern black literature.

Lehmann-Haupt, Christopher. "Books of the Times." *New York Times* 2 April 1992: B2.

Lepow, Lauren. "Paradise Lost and Found: Dualism and Edenic Myth in Toni Morrison's *Tar Baby*." *Contemporary Literature* 28 (Fall, 1987): 363-77. Shows aspects of the Eden story at work in *Tar Baby*, with some emphasis on her use of the idea of dualism.

Lewis, Vashti Crutcher. "African Tradition in Toni Morrison's *Sula*." *Wild Women in the Whirlwind: Afra-American Culture and the Contemporary Literary Renaissance*. Ed. by Joanne M. Braxton and Andree Nicola McLaughlin. New Brunswick, N. J.: Rutgers University Press, 1990. 316-25. Makes the case that Morrison chooses to write from an African point of view, especially in *Sula*.

Lounsberry, Barbara, and Grace Ann Hovet. "Principles of Perception in Toni Morrison's *Sula.*" *Black American Literature Forum* 13 (1979): 126-29. Places the discussion in the context of the question of how black writers deal with the question of perception of the past and the future. Shows that Morrison employs this ordering principle in *Sula.*

Lupton, Mary Jane. "Clothes and Closure in Three Novels by Black Women." *Black American Literature Forum* 20 (1986): 409-21. Considers Morrison's use of "suggestive" clothing in her first three novels. Shows how she contrasts clothing and nature ironically.

McKethan, Lucinda H. "Names to Bear Witness: The Theme and Tradition of Naming in Toni Morrison's *Song of Solomon.*" *CEA Critic* 49 (Winter-Summer, 1986-87): 199-207. Focuses on Morrison's deliberate concern with names of the characters in *Song of Solomon*, particularly with relation to the Afro-American experience of naming.

Magnes, Patricia. "The Knights and the Princess: The Structure of Courtly Love in Toni Morrison's *Tar Baby.*" *South Atlantic Review* 54 (November, 1989): 85-99. Applies the courtly love tradition to a reading of *Tar Baby.*

Marshall, Brenda. "The Gospel According to Pilate." *American Literature* 57 (1985): 486-89. Shows Pilate to be a protean character who plays various roles for the sake of other people.

Martin, Odette. *"Sula." First World* 1 (1977): 34-44. Takes up as the main point of discussion the life as it is found in the Bottoms of *Sula.*

Mason, Theodore O. Jr. "The Novelist as Conservator: Stories and Comprehension in Toni Morrison's *Song of Solomon.*" *Contemporary Literature* 29 (Winter, 1988): 564-81. Looks at the use of stories within the story of *Song of Solomon.*

Mickleson, Anne Z. "Toni Morrison." *Reaching Out: Sensitivity and Order in Recent American Fiction by Women.* Metuchen, N. J.: Scarecrow Press, 1979. 124-53. Concentrates on the quest and "earth mother" issues found in Morrison's earlier work.

Middleton, Victoria. "Sula: An Experimental Life." *C. L. A. Journal* 28 (1985): 367-81. Analyzes Sula's character, arguing that she is an existential kind of hero whose example influences the way others see the world.

Miller, Adam D. "Breedlove, Peace and the Dead." *Black Scholar* (1978): 47-50. Gives an appreciative look at Morrison's work, touching on her most striking aspects.

Minakawa, Harue. "The Motif of Sweetness in Toni Morrison's *Song of Solomon.*" *Kyushu American Literature* 26 (October, 1985): 47-56. Looks at one of the prominent motifs appearing in *Song of Solomon.*

Miner, Madonne M. "Lady No Longer Sings the Blues: Rape, Madness, and Silence in *The Bluest Eye.*" *Conjuring: Black Women Fiction and Literary Tradition.* Ed. by Marjorie Pryse and Hortense J. Spillers. Bloomington: Indiana University Press, 1985. 176-91. Compares Pecola and Philomela in context of considering the theme of female violation.

Mobeley, Marilyn E. "Narrative Dilemma: Jadine as Cultural Orphan in Toni Morrison's *Tar Baby.*" *Southern Review* 23 (Autumn, 1987): 761-77. Focuses on Jadine's becoming cut off from her culture in *Tar Baby.*

Montgomery, M. I. "A Pilgrimage to the Origins: The Apocalypse as Structure and Theme in Toni Morrison's *Sula.*" *Black American Literature Forum* 23 (Spring, 1989): 127-37. Analyzes the distinctly apocalyptical structure and theme found in *Sula.*

Morey, Ann-Janine. "Toni Morrison and the Color of Life." *Christian Century* 16 November 1988: 1039-43. Provides an overview of Morrison's main concerns.

Munro, C. Lynn. "The Tattooed Heart and Serpentine Eye: Morrison's Choice of an Epigraph for *Sula.*" *Black American Literature Forum* 18 (Winter, 1984): 150-54. Provides a critical insight on the appropriateness of the epigraph used in *Sula.*

Myers, Linda Buck; Neil Mahadate, response; Marco A. Portales, response; Richard I. Hernstadt, response. "Perception and Power Through Naming: Characters in Search of a Self in the Fiction of Toni Morrison." *Explorations in Ethnic Studies: Journal of the National Association for Ethnic Studies* 1 (January, 1984): 39-55. Considers the self-discovery question related to the chosen names found in Morrison's fiction.

Nichols, Julie. "Patterns in Toni Morrison's Novels." *English Journal* 72 (1983): 46-48. Points out Morrison's use of appropriate forms and patterns as an aid for those who wish to teach Morrison's novels effectively to high school students.

O'Brien, Edna. "The Clearest Eye: *Jazz.*" *New York Times Book Review* 5 April 1992: 30.

Ogunyemi, Chiwenye. "Order and Disorder in Toni Morrison's *The Bluest Eye.*" *Critique* 19 (1977): 112-20. Looks at the structure and tragic patterns found in Morrison's first novel, considering along the way some of its weak and some of its strong points.

—. "*Sula*: 'A Nigger Joke.'" *Black American Literature Forum* 13 (1979): 130-34. Reveals the ironies in the text of *Sula*, stressing the lives of the characters while concluding that the novel embodies a humorous joke that runs through the town.

Ordonez, Elizabeth J. "Narrative Texts by Ethnic Women: Rereading the Past, Reshaping the Future." *Melus* 9 (Winter, 1982): 19-28. Considers Morrison's kind of narrative in the context of discussing writing by ethnic women writers and how they deal with the past and the future in their works.

Pettis, Joyce. "Difficult Survival: Mothers and Daughters in *The Bluest Eye.*" *Sage* 4 (Fall, 1987): 26-29. Considers the difficult relationship between mothers and daughters in Morrison's first novel.

Portales, Marco. "Toni Morrison's *The Bluest Eye*: Shirley Temple and Cholly." *Centennial Review* 30 (1986): 496-506. Studies the unstable, wounded personality of the protagonist.

Pullin, Faith. "Landscapes of Reality: The Fiction of Contemporary Afro-American Women." *Black Fiction: New Studies in the Afro-American Novel Since 1945.* Ed. by Robert A. Lee. New York: Barnes and Noble, 1980. 173-203. Analyzes *The Bluest Eye* and *Sula*, emphasizing ways in which the two novels break new ground in dealing with black women characters.

Rabinowitz, Paula. "Naming, Magic, and Documentary: The Subversion of the Narrative in *Song of Solomon, Ceremony,* and *China Men.*" *Feminist Re-Visions: What Has Been and Might Be.* Ed. by Vivian Patraha and Louise A. Tilly. Ann Arbor: University of Michigan Press, 1983. 26-42. Discusses the subversive narrative aspects of *Song of Solomon*, while also looking at two other related works by other writers.

Randolph, Laura B. "The Magic of Toni Morrison." *Ebony* July 1988: 100, 102, 104, 108. Provides a look at Morrison's life and poses some questions about her views of her success.

Reddy, Maureen T. "The Tripled Plot and Center of *Sula.*" *Black American Literature Forum* 22 (Spring, 1988): 29-45. Considers the complex plot strategy used in *Sula*.

Reed, Harry. "Toni Morrison, *Song of Solomon,* and Black Cultural Nationalism." *Centennial Review* 32 (Winter, 1988): 50-64. Looks at *Song of Solomon* in the light of black cultural pride and the question of black nationalism.

Reyes, Angelita. "Ancient Properties in the New World: The Paradox of the 'Other' in Toni Morrison's *Tar Baby.*" *Black Scholar* 17 (March-April, 1986): 19-25. Considers Morrison's involvement in questions of old world culture and history.

Rosenberg, Ruth. "'And the Children May Know Their Names': Toni Morrison's *Song of Solomon.*" *Literary Onomastic Studies* 8 (1981): 195-219. Frames the discussion of *Song of Solomon* by considering the importance of knowing one's true name and thus true self.

—. "Seeds in the Hard Ground: Black Girlhood in *The Bluest Eye.*" *Black American Literature Forum* 21 (1987): 435-45. Explores the unique revelations of black girlhood in Morrison's first novel.

Royster, Philip M. "*The Bluest Eye.*" *First World* 1 (1977): 34-44. Shows the relation between the community's values and the characters.

—. "Milkman's Flying: The Scapegoat Transcended in Toni Morrison's *Song of Solomon.*" *C. L. A. Journal* 24 (1981): 419-40. Shows Milkman as a victim and scapegoat, concluding that he develops finally to the point where he stops being such a passive character.

—. "A Priest and a Witch Against the Spiders and the Snakes: Scapegoating in Toni Morrison's *Sula.*" *UMOJA: Scholarly Journal of Black Studies* 2 (1978): 149-68. Reveals Sula and Shadrack as scapegoat figures in *Sula*.

Samuels, Wilfred D. "Liminality and the Search for Self in Toni Morrison's *Song of Solomon.*" *Minority Voices* 5 (Spring-Fall, 1981): 59-68. Follows the self-identification route laid out in *Song of Solomon*.

Sargent, Robert. "A Way of Ordering Experience: A Study of Toni Morrison's *The Bluest Eye* and *Sula*." *Faith of a (Woman) Writer*. Ed. by William McBrien. Westport, Connecticut: Greenwood Press, 1988. 229-36. Focuses on Morrison's first two novels, showing how she tends to organize around the interplay of characters who embody clashing values.

Schapiro, Barbara. "The Bonds of Love and the Boundaries of Self in Toni Morrison's *Beloved*." *Contemporary Literature* 32 (Summer, 1991): 194-210. Argues that *Beloved* is primarily concerned with the problem of recognizing and claiming one's individual existence, with the story showing how this necessary subjectivity can't be achieved apart from the social environment.

Scruggs, Charles. "The Nature of Desire in Toni Morrison's *Song of Solomon*." *Arizona Quarterly* 38 (Winter, 1982): 311-35. Shows the importance of desire in shaping the characters in *Song of Solomon*.

Shannon, Anna. "'We Was Girls Together': A Study of Toni Morrison's *Sula*." *Midwestern Miscellany* 10 (1982) 9-22. Concentrates on the two female protagonists and their special relationship in *Sula*.

Skerrett, Joseph T. Jr. "Recitation to the Griot: Storytelling and Learning in Toni Morrison's *Song of Solomon*." *Conjuring: Black Women Fiction and Literary Tradition*. Ed. by Marjorie Pryse and Hortense J. Spillers. Bloomington: University of Indiana Press, 1985. 195-202. Takes up Morrison's employment of the story-teller's gift, with a discussion of how story-telling functions in the narrative, and with special emphasis given to Pilate's particular gift in this regard.

Smith, Barbara. "Beautiful, Needed, Mysterious." *Freedomways* 14 (1974): 69-72. Undertakes to reveal the mascon images used in *Sula*. Praises Morrison for making readers feel the connection between black women who share their lives with others.

Smith, Valerie. "The Quest for and Discovery of Identity in Toni Morrison's *Song of Solomon*." *Southern Review* 21 (1985): 721-32. Traces Milkman's process of education, stressing the connection between one's social role and self-discovery. Special focus is placed on the novel's structure and thematic deliberations.

—. "Toni Morrison's Narratives of Community." *Self Discovery and Authority in Afro-American Narrative*. Cambridge, Massachusetts: Harvard University Press, 1987. 122-53. Concentrates on Morrison's presentation of community in her first three novels. Also undertakes to explain her use of narrative process and her use of knowing the past as a means of self-discovery.

Spallino, Chiara. "*Song of Solomon*: An Adventure in Structure." *Callaloo* 8 (1985): 510-24. Gives the opinion that *Song of Solomon* shows how important it is for blacks to hold on to their identity.

Spillers, Hortense J. "A Hateful Passion, A Love Lost." *Feminist Issues in Literary Scholarship*. Ed. by Shari Bernstock. Bloomington: Indiana University Press, 1987. Compares *Sula* with two other novels by black women writers in the context of discussing the progression of black women.

Stein, Karen F. "'I Didn't Even Know His Name': Names and Naming in Toni Morrison's *Sula*." *Names* (1980): 226-29. Takes up Morrison's symbolic use of names, with the discussion related to the main thematic point that all the characters wind up in irremediable loneliness.

—. "Toni Morrison's *Sula*: A Black Woman's Epic." *Black American Literature Forum* 18 (1984): 146-50. Shows *Sula* to be a break-through epic, focusing on what the two main characters learn during the course of the story.

Steiner, Wendy. "The Clearest Eye: *Playing in the Dark*." *New York Times Book Review* 5 April 1992: 17.

Stepto, Robert. *From Behind the Veil: A Study of Afro-American Narrative*. Urbana: University of Illinois Press, 1979. Takes an overview of Morrison's earlier writing.

Story, R. "An Excursion Into the Black World: The Seven Days in Toni Morrison's *Song of Solomon*." *Black American Literature Forum* 23 (Spring, 1989): 149-58. Focuses on the world particularly represented by Guitar in *Song of Solomon*.

Strouse, Jean. "Toni Morrison's Black Magic." *Newsweek* 30 March 1981: 52-57. Surveys Morrison's life and career and gives an early review of *Tar Baby*. Notes that in this novel she makes certain advances.

Tegnor, Eleanor Q. "Toni Morrison's Pecola: A Portrait in Pathos." *MAWA Review* 1 (Spring, 1982): 24-27. Concentrates on the sad truths of the central character's life in Morrison's first novel.

Turner, Darwin T. "Theme, Characterization, and Style in the Works of Toni Morrison." *Black Women Writers (1950-1980)*. Ed. by Mari Evans. New York: Doubleday, 1984. 361-70. Makes the case that Morrison is so effective in the use of traditional elements of fiction that she must be considered a major writer.

Umeh, Marie A. "A Comparative Study of the Idea of Motherhood in Two Third World Novels." *C. L. A. Journal* 31 (September, 1987): 31-43. Provides a comparison of how Morrison and Buchi Emecheta strive to write realistically about the experiences of black women.

Wagner, Linda W. "Toni Morrison: Mastery of Narrative." *Contemporary American Women Writers: Narrative Strategies*. Ed. by Catherine Rainwater and William Scherch. Lexington: University Press of Kentucky, 1985. 191-207. Discusses Morrison's narrative techniques, specifically the organization and design in her first four novels.

Warner, Anne Bradford. "New Myths and Ancient Properties: The Fiction of Toni Morrison." *Hollins Critic* 25 (June, 1988): 1-11. Considers the use of myths and folklore characteristic of Morrison's fiction.

Wedertz-Furtado, Utelinda. "Historical Dimensions in Toni Morrison's *Song of Solomon*." *History and Tradition in Afro-American Culture*. Ed. by Gunter H. Lenz. Frankfurt, Germany: Campus, 1984. 222-241. Emphasizes the historical foundations of Morrison's fiction.

Wegs, Joyce M. "Toni Morrison's *Song of Solomon*: A Blues Song." *Essays in Literature* 9 (1982): 211-23. Points out the blues-like effectiveness of Morrison's fiction, focusing on the sources of and reasons for singing the blues in this story, and finally suggesting that the presence of the blues can inspire and uplift the characters.

Weixlman, Joe. "Culture Clash, Survival, and Transformation." *Mississippi Quarterly* 38 (1984-85): 21-32. Points to the apparent influence of South American magical reality on Morrison.

Wessling, Joseph H. "Narcissism in Toni Morrison's *Sula*." *C. L. A. Journal* 31 (March, 1988): 281-98. Analyzes the issue of narcissism as it applies to *Sula*.

Willis, Susan. "I Shop Therefore I Am: Is There a Place for Afro-American Culture in Commodity Culture?" *Changing Our Own Words: Essays on Criticism, Theory, and Writing by Black Women*. Ed. by Cheryl Wall. New Brunswick, N. J.: Rutgers University Press, 1989. 173-95. Contrasts the question of an Afro-American identity with the prevalent American culture.

—. "Eruptions of Funk: Historicizing Toni Morrison." *Specifying: Black Women Writing: The American Experience*. Madison: University of Wisconsin Press, 1987. 83-109. Investigates how Morrison writes about the intrusion of the past into the present in her first four books.

—. "Eruptions of Funk: Historicizing Toni Morrison." *Black American Literature Forum* 16 (1982): 34-41. Same content as in above entry.

Toni Morrison Bibliographies

Alexander, Harriet S. "Toni Morrison: An Annotated Bibliography of Critical Articles and Essays, 1975-84." *C. L. A. Journal* 33 (1989): 81-93. Gives annotated listings focusing on Morrison's most productive decade.

Fikes, Robert Jr. "Echoes from Small Town Ohio: A Toni Morrison Bibliography." *Obsidian* 5 (1979): 142-48. Offers an early and thus limited bibliography.

Martin, Curtis. "A Bibliography of Writings by Toni Morrison." *Contemporary American Women Writers: Narrative Strategies*. Lexington: University Press of Kentucky, 1985. 205-207. Offers a selected bibliography.

Middleton, David I. *Toni Morrison: An Annotated Bibliography*. New York: Garland, 1987. Provides the most comprehensive bibliography currently available on Morrison.

Index